Madder

anthology I /CAMILLA, SIBELLA, IMOGEN, & BEATRICE

knit patterns and photography by
Carrie Bostick Hoge

photography, styling, and book design
by carrie bostick hoge

isbn 9780692239780

published by madder

10 9 8 7 6 5 4 3

printed in china

table *of* contents

CAMILLA

S

SIBELLA

I

IMOGEN

B

BEATRICE

Welcome...

Madder's *Anthology 1* is a collection of four unique stitch stories: Camilla, with a cascading fan pattern; Sibella, with rows of pretty floral lace; Imogen, elegant with petals and faggot stich in constant harmony; and Beatrice, with its interesting elongated stitches that are crossed over one another, creating beauty and intrigue.

It all began in 2010—a big year for me. In January of that year, I began working on the launch of Quince & Co., a yarn company owned by Pam Allen. The company started with only four yarns and so I became familiar with each one quickly. By working with a minimal amount of yarns, and due to the beautiful stitch definition each yarn achieved, I was able to focus on the stitches and developed a style and a voice I hadn't yet found. A lot of swatching occured in the first 3 months of 2010! Also, in the spring of 2010, I became pregnant with my daughter. Hence the beginning of my designs for babies and kids.

One of the garments I designed for the premiere collection of Quince & Co. was Annabel, a simple garter stitch pullover worked in cushy, soft Osprey yarn. I had long loved garter stitch, but this sweater really struck a chord with me and I wanted to push it further. I had always been drawn to the flow of the fan pattern and really liked the idea that the garter stitch would work its way from the body to the center panel without interuption. And with one swatch I was sold and Camilla was created. The mama and baby patterns were the first to be released. Later came the kid, then the blanket. And for this book I designed a crescent-shaped shawl in two different yarn weights.

Imogen was actually the next up in the timeline, released in 2011, though it appears third in this book. The story was developed out of a sheer obsession with Frost Flowers. The stitch appears on the cover of Barbara Walker's book, *A Treasury of Knitting Patterns,* and I know many designers have used it before me and many will use it in the future, but that didn't stop me. Not for one minute. The stitch pattern is absolutely appealing to knit and irresistibly gorgeous to look at. I got carried away and designed my first little collection, Imogen & Immie, named after my daughter. For this book, I added Imogen Spring with its lovely sleeve length that hits just above the elbow.

Shortly after Imogen, in the spring of 2012, I released Sibella Pullover. Since I just couldn't let go of Frost Flowers completely, I pulled the leaf motif out and worked this into a linear pattern with stockinette stitch rows in between. I love how the flowers dance around the yoke of the pullover! Sibella Scarf was designed and knitted around the same time, but never officially released until now. Also, specially made for this book are Sibella Cardigan and Cowl to make the story complete.

And last but not least is Lady Beatrice. I had had my eye on the *Indian Cross Stitch* for a while (also from Walker's book) and finally swatched this first in 2012. I tried it in all different weights of yarns and found that fingering to worsted worked best. I especially loved how it looked in worsted weight— you really get to see those strands of the yarn crossing over each other. Of course, you know I love its use of garter stitch, but another brilliant aspect is that it is, for the most part, reversible. Perfect for scarves, cowls, wraps, and drapey cardis that fold over slightly.

These stitch patterns and designs included in *Anthology 1* embody what I love about knitting— beauty, movement, and intrigue through stitches.

I hope you enjoy them, too.

Carrie

CAMILLA

camilla pullover

camilla shawl light

camilla shawl

camilla kid, camilla babe & camilla blanket

SIBELLA

sibella cardigan

sibella cowl

sibella pullover

sibella scarf

IMOGEN

imogen tee

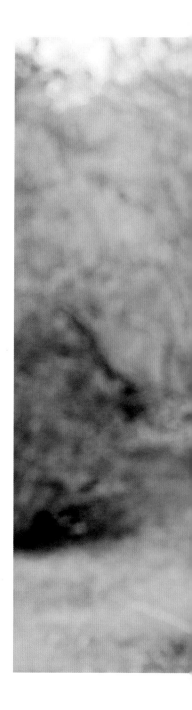

imogen spring

immie blanket & immie tee

BEATRICE

beatrice cardigan

bea cardi

beatrice wrap

beatrice scarf

bea tee

the PATTERNS

camilla pullover

Finished Bust Measurements

30¼ (33½, 37, 40½, 43¾, 47¼)"
Shown in size: 33½"

Yarn

Osprey by Quince & Co. (100% American wool;
170 yds [155 m]/100g)
• 4 (5, 5, 6, 7, 7) skeins in Sedum
OR 770 (840, 905, 1085, 1180, 1270) yds aran
weight yarn

Needles

• One 16" circular (circ) needle in size US 10½
  [6.5mm]
• One 29" circ in size US 10½ [6.5mm]
• One set dpns in size US 10½ [6.5mm]

Or size needed to obtain gauge

Notions

• Stitch markers in two colors
• Tapestry needle for weaving in ends
• Waste yarn for holding sts

Gauge

14 sts and 26 rnds = 4" in garter st, blocked.

Fan Pattern (panel of 25 sts)

(Also, see chart page 51)

Rnd 1: P1, yo, [k1, p1] 11 times, k1, yo, p1—
27 sts.
Rnd 2: K2, [k1, p1] 11 times, k3.
Rnd 3: P2, yo, [k1, p1] 11 times, k1, yo, p2—
29 sts.
Rnd 4: K3, [k1, p1] 11 times, k4.
Rnd 5: P3, yo, [k1, p1] 11 times, k1, yo, p3—
31 sts.
Rnd 6: K4, [k1, p1] 11 times, k5.
Rnd 7: P4, yo, [k1, p1] 11 times, k1, yo, p4—
33 sts.
Rnd 8: K5, [k1, p1] 11 times, k6.
Rnd 9: P5, yo, [k1, p1] 11 times, k1, yo, p5—
35 sts.

Rnd 10: K6, [k1, p1] 11 times, k7.
Rnd 11: P6, yo, [k1, p1] 11 times, k1, yo, p6—
37 sts.
Rnd 12: K7, [k1, p1] 11 times, k8.
Rnd 13: P7, [ssk] 5 times, sl—k2tog—psso, [k2tog]
5 times, p7—25 sts.
Rnd 14: Knit.
Rep Rnds 1—14 for Fan Pattern.

Notes

1. Pattern requires 4 stitch markers to indicate raglan
shaping and 2 markers to indicate stitches worked in
Fan Pattern. Use a different color to mark Fan Pattern
stitches.
2. Stitch count changes every other rnd in Fan Pattern.

Pullover

Body
With longer circ and using the long-tail cast on, CO 106 (118, 130, 142, 154, 166) sts. Place marker (pm) for BOR and join to work in the rnd, being careful not to twist sts.

Begin garter stitch and Fan Pattern
First rnd *place markers:* P14 (17, 20, 23, 26, 29) sts for front, pm, work Rnd 1 of Fan Pattern over 25 sts, pm, p14 (17, 20, 23, 26, 29) for front, pm, p53 (59, 65, 71, 77, 83) sts for back.
Next rnd: K14 (17, 20, 23, 26, 29) sts, sl m, work Rnd 2 of Fan Pattern, sl m, k14 (17, 20, 23, 26, 29), sl m, k53 (59, 65, 71, 77, 83) sts to end.

Work as est until pc meas approx 13¼ (13, 12¼, 14¼, 13½, 13¼)" from beg, ending after Rnd 14 (12, 8, 6, 2, 14) of Fan Pattern.

Begin underarm bind-off
Next rnd: Work as est to 3 sts before BOR marker. BO 6 sts knitwise, removing BOR marker.
Next rnd: Work as est to 3 sts before side marker, BO 6 sts knitwise, removing side marker, work as est to end—11 (14, 17, 20, 23, 26) sts rem each side of Fan Pattern on front; 47 (53, 59, 65, 71, 77) sts rem on back.

Keep sts on circ; do not break yarn. Set aside.

Sleeves
With dpns and using the long-tail cast on, CO 40 (42, 44, 48, 52, 56) sts. Pm for BOR and join to work in the rnd, being careful not to twist sts.

Begin garter stitch
First rnd: Purl.
Next rnd: Knit.
Cont in garter st in the rnd until pc meas 12 (12, 12½, 12½, 13, 13)" from beg, ending after a knit rnd.

Begin underarm bind-off
Next rnd: Purl to 3 sts before m, BO 6 sts knitwise, removing m—34 (36, 38, 42, 46, 50) sts rem.
Next rnd: Knit to end.

Slip sts to waste yarn; break yarn. Set aside.

Yoke
Join sleeve stitches to body
Note: As you proceed with the yoke, continue working Fan Pattern between markers as est, all other stitches are worked in garter st in the rnd.

With body sts still on circ, pm for BOR, p34 (36, 38, 42, 46, 50) sleeve sts to yoke, pm, p11 (14, 17, 20, 23, 26) front stitches to first m, work Rnd 3 (1, 11, 9, 5, 3) of Fan Pattern, p11 (14, 17, 20, 23, 26) front sts, pm, p34 (36, 38, 42, 46, 50) sleeve sts to yoke, pm, p47 (53, 59, 65, 71, 77) back sts to end.

Work 2 rnds even, ending after a purl rnd.

Begin yoke shaping
Next rnd *dec rnd:* *K1, k2tog, work to 2 sts before m, ssk, sl m; rep from * 3 times—8 sts dec'd.

Rep *dec rnd* every 4th rnd 3 (3, 3, 3, 3, 2) times, then every other rnd 9 (10, 12, 13, 15, 18) times, changing to shorter circ when necessary.

Cont even as est until Rnd 13 of Fan Pattern is completed—58 (66, 66, 78, 82, 86) sts rem.

Next rnd: BO all sts knitwise on Rnd 14 of Fan Pattern.

Finishing
Sew underarm seams. Block pc to measurements.

camilla pullover

Key

☐	knit
⊟	purl
⊡	yo
◺	ssk
◪	sl—k2tog—psso
◿	k2tog
■	no stitch

Fan Pattern chart

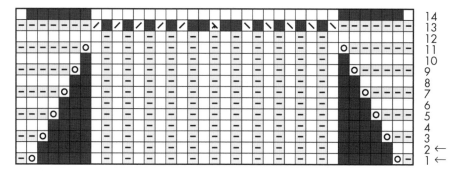

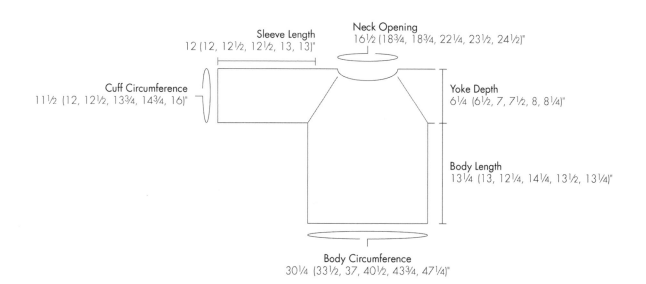

Sleeve Length
12 (12, 12½, 12½, 13, 13)"

Neck Opening
16½ (18¾, 18¾, 22¼, 23½, 24½)"

Cuff Circumference
11½ (12, 12½, 13¾, 14¾, 16)"

Yoke Depth
6¼ (6½, 7, 7½, 8, 8¼)"

Body Length
13¼ (13, 12¼, 14¼, 13½, 13¼)"

Body Circumference
30¼ (33½, 37, 40½, 43¾, 47¼)"

camilla shawl light

Finished Measurements
73" long x 6¾" high

Yarn
Primo Fingering by The Plucky Knitter (75% merino, 20% cashmere, 5% nylon; 385 yds [352 m]/100g)
- 2 skeins in Macaron

OR 575 yds fingering weight yarn

Needles
- One 32" or longer circular needle (circ) in size US 5 [3.75 mm]

Or size needed to obtain gauge

Notions
- Tapestry needle for weaving in ends

Gauge
22 sts and 46 rows = 4" in garter st, blocked.

Note
Stitch count changes every other row in Fan Pattern.

Fan Pattern (multiple of 16 sts + 1)
(Also, see chart page 53)

Row 1: (RS) K1, *yo, [k1, p1] 7 times, k1, yo, k1; rep from * to end.

Row 2: K2, *[p1, k1] 7 times, p1, k3; rep from * across, end last repeat k2.

Row 3: K2, *yo, [k1, p1] 7 times, k1, yo, k3; rep from * across, end last repeat k2.

Row 4: K3, *[p1, k1] 7 times, p1, k5; rep from * across, end last repeat k3.

Row 5: K3, *yo, [k1, p1] 7 times, k1, yo, k5; rep from * across, end last repeat k3.

Row 6: K4, *[p1, k1] 7 times, p1, k7; rep from * across, end last repeat k4.

Row 7: K4, *yo, [k1, p1] 7 times, k1, yo, k7; rep from * across, end last repeat k4.

Row 8: K5, [p1, k1] 7 times, p1, k9; rep from * across, end last repeat k5.

Row 9: K5, *[ssk] 3 times, sl 1—k2tog—psso, [k2tog] 3 times, k9 ; rep from * across, end last repeat k7.

Row 10: K5, *p7, k9; rep from * across; end last repeat k5.

Rep Rows 1—10 for Fan Pattern.

Shawl
Using the long-tail cast on, CO 401 sts. Do not join.

Set up row: (WS) K1, *[p1, k1]; rep from * to end.

Begin Fan pattern
Row 1: (RS) Work all sts in Row 1 of Fan Pattern. Cont to work all sts in Rows 2–10 of Fan Pattern one time, then Rows 1–10 one time, then Rows 1–9 one time.

Begin garter stitch
Next row: (WS) Knit.

Next row *dec row:* (RS) K12, *k2tog, k2; rep from * to last 13 sts, k2tog, knit to end (95 sts dec'd)—306 sts.

Work 3 rows in garter st.

Begin short rows
Row 1: (RS) K204 sts, turn.

Row 2: (WS) K102 sts, turn.

Row 3 *dec and short row:* (RS) Knit to 1 st before turning point, k2tog, k4, turn (1 st dec'd)—305 sts.

Row 4 *dec and short row:* (WS) Knit to 1 st before turning point, k2tog, k4, turn (1 st dec'd)—304 sts.

Rep last 2 rows 15 more times—274 sts.

Next row: (RS) Knit to 1 st before turning point, k2tog, knit to end (1 st dec'd)—273 sts.

Next row: (WS) Knit to 1 st before turning point, k2tog, knit to end (1 st dec'd)—272 sts.

Next row: (RS) Loosely BO all sts knitwise.

Finishing
Weave in ends. Wet block pc to measurements.

Fan Pattern chart

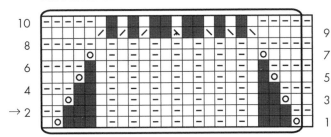

Key

- ☐ knit on RS, purl on WS
- ⊟ purl on RS, knit on WS
- ⊡ yo
- ⊠ ssk
- sl—k2tog—psso
- ⊿ k2tog
- ■ no stitch
- ☐ pattern repeat

camilla shawl

Finished Measurements
60" long x 8" high
Yarn
Primo Worsted by The Plucky Knitter (75% merino, 20% cashmere, 5% nylon; 200 yds [182 m]/100g)
- 2 skeins in Putty in My Hand
OR 400 yds worsted weight yarn
Needles
- One 32" circular needle (circ) or longer in size US 7 [4.5 mm]
Or size needed to obtain gauge
Notions
- Tapestry needle for weaving in ends
Gauge
18 sts and 36 rows = 4" in garter stitch, blocked.

Fan Pattern (multiple of 24 sts + 1)
(Also, see chart page 54)
Row 1: (RS) K1, *yo, [k1 p1] 11 times, k1, yo, k1; rep from * to end.
Row 2: K2, *[p1, k1] 11 times, p1, k3; rep from * across, end last repeat k2.
Row 3: K2, *yo, [k1, p1] 11 times, k1, yo, k3; rep from * across, end last repeat k2.
Row 4: K3, *[p1, k1] 11 times, p1, k5; rep from * across, end last repeat k3.
Row 5: K3, *yo, [k1, p1] 11 times, k1, yo, k5; rep from * across, end last repeat k3.
Row 6: K4, *[p1, k1] 11 times, p1, k7; rep from * across, end last repeat k4.
Row 7: K4, *yo, [k1, p1] 11 times, k1, yo, k7; rep from * across, end last repeat k4.

Row 8: K5, [p1, k1] 11 times, p1, k9; rep from * across, end last repeat k5.
Row 9: K5, *yo, [k1, p1] 11 times, k1, yo, k9; rep from * across, end last repeat k5.
Row 10: K6, *(p1, k1) 11 times, p1, k11; rep from * across, end last repeat k6.
Row 11: K6, *yo, (k1, p1) 11 times, k1, yo, k11; rep from * across, end last repeat k6.
Row 12: K7, *(p1, k1) 11 times, p1, k13; rep from * across, end last repeat k7.
Row 13: K7, *[ssk] 5 times, sl 1—k2tog—psso, [k2tog] 5 times, k13; rep from * across, end last repeat k7.
Row 14: K7, *p11, k13; rep from * across; end last repeat k7.
Rep Rows 1–14 for Fan Pattern.

Shawl
CO 289 sts. Do not join.

Set up row: (WS) K1, *[p1, k1]; rep from * to end.

Begin Fan Pattern
Row 1: (RS) Work all sts in Row 1 of Fan Pattern. Cont to work all sts in Rows 2–14 one time, then Rows 1–13 one time.

Begin garter stitch
Next row: (WS) Knit.
Next row *dec row:* (RS) K11, *k2, k2tog; rep from * to last 10 sts, knit to end (67 sts dec'd)—222 sts. Work 3 rows in garter st.

Begin short rows
Row 1: (RS) K148 sts, turn.
Row 2: (WS) K74 sts, turn.

Row 3 *dec and short row:* (RS) Knit to 1 st before turning point, k2tog, k4turn (1 st dec'd)—221 sts.
Row 4 *dec and short row:* (WS) Knit to 1 st before turning point, k2tog, k4 turn (1 st dec'd)—220 sts. Rep last 2 rows 13 more times—194 sts.

Next row: (RS) Knit to 1 st before turning point, k2tog, knit to end (1 st dec'd)—193 sts.
Next row: (WS) Knit to 1 st before turning point, k2tog, knit to end (1 st dec'd)—192 sts.

Next row: (RS) Loosely BO all sts knitwise.

Finishing
Weave in ends. Wet block pc to measurements.

Fan Pattern chart

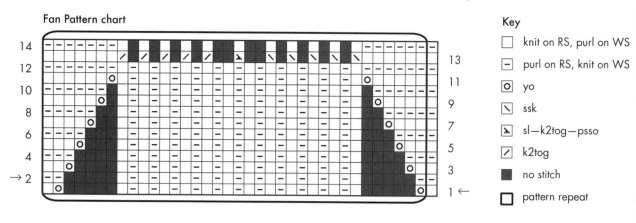

Key
- ☐ knit on RS, purl on WS
- − purl on RS, knit on WS
- ○ yo
- ＼ ssk
- ⅄ sl−k2tog−psso
- ／ k2tog
- ■ no stitch
- ☐ pattern repeat

camilla kid

Finished Chest Measurements
24¼ (26½, 28¾, 30, 31)"
Sizes: 4 (6, 8, 10, 12) years
Shown in size 24¼"
Yarn
Osprey by Quince & Co.
(170 yds [155m] /100g)
- 3 (3, 4, 4, 5) skeins Petal

OR 415 (500, 600, 685, 760) yds aran weight yarn
Needles
- One 16" circular needle (circ) in size US 10½ [6.5mm]
- One set dpns in size US 10½ [6.5mm]

Or size needed to obtain gauge

Notions

- Stitch markers in two colors
- Tapestry needle for weaving in ends
- Waste yarn

Gauge

14 sts and 26 rows = 4" in garter st, blocked.

Fan Pattern (panel of 17 sts)

(Also, see chart page 56)

Rnd 1: P1, yo, [k1, p1] 7 times, k1, yo, p1—
19 sts.
Rnd 2: K2, [k1, p1] 7 times, k3.
Rnd 3: P2, yo, [k1, p1] 7 times, k1, yo, p2—
21 sts.
Rnd 4: K3, [k1, p1] 7 times, k4.
Rnd 5: P3, yo, [k1, p1] 7 times, k1, yo, p3—
23 sts.
Rnd 6: K4, [k1, p1] 7 times, k5.
Rnd 7: P4, yo, [k1, p1] 7 times, k1, yo, p4—
25 sts.
Rnd 8: K5, [k1, p1] 7 times, k6.
Rnd 9: P5, [ssk] 3 times, sl1—k2tog—psso, [k2tog]
3 times, p5—17 sts.
Rnd 10: Knit.
Rep Rnds 1–10 for Fan Pattern.

Notes

1. Pattern requires 4 stitch markers to indicate raglan shaping and 2 markers to indicate stitches worked in Fan Pattern. Use a different color to mark Fan Pattern stitches.
2. Stitch count changes every other rnd in Fan Pattern.

Pullover

Body

With circ and using the long-tail cast on, CO 86 (94, 102, 106, 110) sts. Place marker (pm) for BOR and join to work in the rnd, being careful not to twist sts.

Begin garter stitch and Fan Pattern

First rnd *place markers:* P13 (15, 17, 18, 19) sts for front, pm, work Rnd 1 of Fan Pattern over 17 sts, pm, p13 (15, 17, 18, 19) for front, pm for side, p43 (47, 51, 53, 55) sts for back.
Next rnd: K13 (15, 17, 18, 19) sts, sl m, work Rnd 2 of Fan Pattern, sl m, k13 (15, 17, 18, 19), sl m, k43 (47, 51, 53, 55) sts to end.

Cont as est for 38 (46, 54, 62, 60) more rnds, ending after Rnd 10 (8, 6, 4, 2) of Fan Pattern; body meas approx 6 (7¼, 8¼, 9½, 9¼).

Divide for armholes

Next rnd: Work as est to 2 sts before BOR marker, BO 4 sts knitwise removing BOR m.
Next rnd: Work to 2 sts before side marker, BO 4 sts knitwise, removing marker, work to end of back as est—11 (13, 15, 16, 17) sts rem each side of Fan Pattern on front; 39 (43, 47, 49, 51) sts rem on back. [42 (50, 58, 66, 64) rnds worked to here]

Keep sts on circ; do not break yarn. Set aside.

Sleeves

With dpns and using the long-tail cast on, CO 32 (34, 35, 36, 38) sts. Pm for BOR and join to work in the rnd, being careful not to twist sts.

Begin garter stitch

Next rnd: Purl.
Next rnd: Knit.
Cont in garter st in the rnd until pc meas 6 (7, 8, 9, 10)", ending after a knit rnd.

Begin underarm bind-off

Next rnd: Purl until 2 sts before marker, BO 4 sts knitwise, removing BOR m—28 (30, 31, 32, 34) sts rem.
Next rnd: Knit to end.
Slip sts to waste yarn; break yarn. Set aside.
Repeat for second sleeve.

Yoke

Join sleeve stitches to body

Note: As you proceed with the yoke, continue working Fan Pattern between markers as est, all other stitches are worked in garter st in the rnd.

With body sts still on circ, pm for BOR, p28 (30, 31, 32, 34) sleeve sts to yoke, pm, p11 (13, 15, 16, 17) front sts to first m, work Rnd 3 (1, 9, 7, 5) of Fan Pattern, p11 (13, 15, 16, 17) front sts, pm, p28 (30, 31, 32, 34) sleeve sts to yoke, pm, p39 (43, 47, 49, 51) back sts to end.

Work 2 rnds even, ending after a purl rnd.

Begin raglan shaping

Next rnd *dec rnd:* *K1, k2tog, work to 2 sts before m, ssk, sl m; rep from * three times more—8 sts dec'd. [46 (54, 62, 70, 68) rnds worked to here] Rep *dec rnd* every 4th rnd 8 (8, 7, 8, 8) times, then every other rnd 0 (1, 3, 3, 4) time(s), changing to dpns is necessary. [78 (88, 96, 108, 108) rnds worked to here]

For Size 8 only:

Next rnd *dec rnd body only:* *Work across sleeve sts to m, sl m, k1, k2tog, work as est to 2 sts before next m, ssk, sl m; rep from * one more time—4 sts dec'd. [78 (88, 98, 108, 108) rnds worked to here]

Cont even until Rnd 9 of Fan Pattern is completed—62 (66, 64, 66, 66) sts rem.

Next rnd: Loosely BO all sts knitwise on Rnd 10 of Fan Pattern.

Finishing

Sew underarm seams. Block pc to measurements.

Key

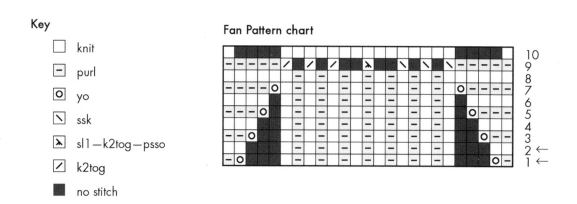

Fan Pattern chart

Sleeve Length
6 (7, 8, 9, 10)"

Neck Opening
17¾ (18¾, 18¼, 18¾, 18¾)"

Cuff Circumference
9¼ (9¾, 10, 10¼, 10¾)"

Yoke Depth
5¾ (6, 6¼, 6½, 7)"

Body Length
6¼ (7½, 8½, 9¾, 9½)"

Body Circumference
24¼ (26½, 28¾, 30, 31)"

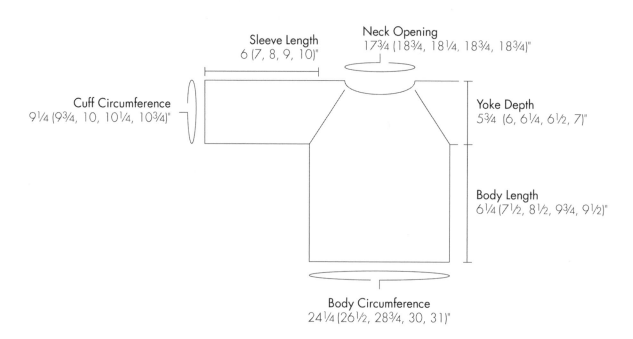

camilla babe

Finished Measurements
18¼ (19, 20¾, 22½, 24¼)"
Sizes: 3 months (6 m, 12 m, 24 m, 3 years)
Shown in size 18¼"

Yarn
Lark by Quince & Co.
(100% American wool; 134 yds [123 m]/50g)
• 3 (3, 4, 4, 5) skeins in Frost or Egret
OR 310 (360, 445, 520, 570) yds in worsted weight yarn

Needles
• One 16" circular needle (circ) in size US 7 [4.5 mm]
• One set dpns in size US 7 [4.5 mm]
Or size needed to obtain gauge

Notions
• Stitch markers in two colors
• Tapestry needle for weaving in ends
• Waste yarn

Gauge
19 sts and 40 rnds = 4" in garter st, blocked.

Fan Pattern (panel of 17 sts)
(Also, see chart page 56)
Rnd 1: P1, yo, [k1, p1] 7 times, k1, yo, p1—19 sts.
Rnd 2: K2, [k1, p1] 7 times, k3.
Rnd 3: P2, yo, [k1, p1] 7 times, k1, yo, p2—21 sts.
Rnd 4: K3, [k1, p1] 7 times, k4.
Rnd 5: P3, yo, [k1, p1] 7 times, k1, yo, p3—23 sts.
Rnd 6: K4, [k1, p1] 7 times, k5.
Rnd 7: P4, yo, [k1, p1] 7 times, k1, yo, p4—25 sts.
Rnd 8: K5, [k1, p1] 7 times, k6.
Rnd 9: P5, [ssk] 3 times, sl1-k2tog-psso, [k2tog] 3 times, p5—17 sts.
Rnd 10: Knit.
Rep Rnds 1—10 for Fan Pattern.

Notes
1. Pattern requires 4 stitch markers to indicate raglan shaping and 2 markers to indicate stitches worked in Fan Pattern. Use a different color to mark Fan Pattern stitches.
2. Stitch count changes every other rnd in Fan Pattern.

Pullover
Body
With circ and using the long-tail cast on, CO 86 (90, 98, 106,114) sts. Place marker (pm) for BOR and join to work in the rnd, being careful not to twist sts.

Begin garter stitch and Fan Pattern
First rnd *place markers:* P13 (14, 16, 18, 20) sts for front, pm, work Rnd 1 of Fan Pattern over 17 sts, pm, p13 (14, 16, 18, 20) sts for front, pm for side, p43 (45, 49, 53, 57) sts for back.

Next rnd: K13 (14, 16, 18, 20) sts for front, sl m, work Rnd 2 of Fan Pattern, sl m, k13 (14, 16,18, 20) sts for front, sl m for side, k43 (45, 49, 53, 57) sts to end.

Work as est for 40 (38, 40, 46, 56) more rnds, ending after Rnd 2 (10, 2, 8, 8) of Fan Pattern; body meas approx 4¼ (4, 4¼, 4¾, 5¾)" from beg.

Begin underarm bind-off
Next rnd: Work as est to 2 (2, 2, 2, 3) sts before BOR marker, BO 4 (4, 4, 4, 6) sts knitwise, removing BOR marker.

Next rnd: Work as est to 2 (2, 2, 2, 3) sts before side marker, BO 4 (4, 4, 4, 6) sts knitwise, removing side marker, knit to end—11 (12, 14, 16, 17) sts rem each side of Fan Pattern on front; 39 (41, 45, 49, 51) sts rem on back. [44 (42, 44, 50, 60) rnds worked to here]

Keep sts on circ; do not break yarn. Set aside.

Sleeves

With dpns and using the long-tail cast on, CO 34 (38, 42, 44, 44) sts. Divide sts evenly over dpns. Pm for BOR and join to work in the rnd.

Begin garter stitch

Rnd 1: Purl.
Rnd 2: Knit.

Cont in garter st in the rnd until sleeve meas 4 (5, 5½, 6, 6)" from beg, ending after a knit rnd.

Begin underarm bind-off

Next rnd: Purl until 2 (2, 2, 2, 3) sts before BOR marker, BO 4 (4, 4, 4, 6) sts knitwise—30 (34, 38, 40, 38) sts rem.

Next rnd: Knit to end.

Slip sts to waste yarn; break yarn. Set aside.
Repeat for second sleeve.

Yoke

Join sleeve stitches to body

Note: As you proceed with the yoke, continue working Fan Pattern between markers as est, all other stitches are worked in garter st in the rnd.

With body sts still on circ, pm for BOR, transfer 30 (34, 38, 40, 38) held sleeve sts onto needle and purl across, pm, p11 (12, 14, 16, 17) front sts to first Fan Pattern m, sl m, work Rnd 5 (3, 5, 1, 1) of Fan Pattern, to next Fan Pattern m, sl m, p11 (12, 14, 16, 17) rem front sts, pm, transfer 30 (34, 38, 40, 38) held sleeve sts onto needle and purl across, pm, p39 (41, 45, 49, 51) back sts to end—144 (154, 172, 180, 180) sts.

Work 0 (0, 2, 2, 2) rnds even.

Begin raglan shaping

Next rnd *dec rnd:* *K1, k2tog, work to 2 sts before m, ssk, sl m; rep from * 3 more times (8 sts dec'd). [46 (44, 48, 54, 64) rnds worked to here]

Rep *dec rnd* every 4th rnd 8 (8, 10, 11, 11) times more, then every other rnd 0 (1, 0, 0, 0) time(s), changing to dpns if necessary, ending after Rnd 8 of Fan Pattern. [78 (78, 88, 98, 108) rnds worked to here]

Work 1 rnd even, ending after Rnd 9 of Fan Pattern—66 (70, 78, 82, 82) sts rem.

Next rnd: Loosely BO all sts knitwise.

Finishing

Weave in ends. Sew underarm seams. Steam or wet block pc to measurements.

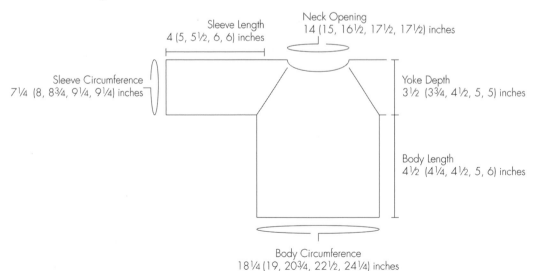

Sleeve Length
4 (5, 5½, 6, 6) inches

Neck Opening
14 (15, 16½, 17½, 17½) inches

Sleeve Circumference
7¼ (8, 8¾, 9¼, 9¼) inches

Yoke Depth
3½ (3¾, 4½, 5, 5) inches

Body Length
4½ (4¼, 4½, 5, 6) inches

Body Circumference
18¼ (19, 20¾, 22½, 24¼) inches

camilla blanket

Finished Measurements
Approx 30" wide x 28½" high

Yarn
Osprey by Quince & Co.
(100% American wool; 170 yds [155 m]/100g)
• 4 skeins in Clay
OR 680 yds aran weight yarn

Needles
• One 24" circular (circ) needle in size US 10½
[6.5mm]

Or size needed to obtain gauge

Notions
• Tapestry needle for weaving in ends

Gauge
14 sts and 27 rows = 4" in garter st, blocked.

Notes
1. Blanket is worked with circular needles to accommodate large number of stitches. Blanket is worked back and forth in rows.
2. Stitch count changes every other row in stitch pattern.
3. Stitch repeat is a multiple of 24 +1.

Blanket
Using the long-tail cast on, CO 113 sts. Do not join.

Begin garter stitch edge
First row: (WS) Knit.
Cont in garter st for 12 more rows, ending after a RS row.

Next row set up row: (WS) K8, (k1, p1) until 9 sts rem, k9.

Begin Fan Pattern
(Also, see chart page 60)
Row 1: (RS) K9, *yo, [k1, p1] 11 times, k1, yo, k1; rep from * to last 8 sts, k8—121 sts.

Row 2: K9, *p2, [k1, p1] 11 times, p1, k1; rep from * to last 8 sts, k8.
Row 3: K10, *yo, [k1, p1] 11 times, k1, yo, k3; rep from * across, end last repeat k10—129 sts.
Row 4: K10, *p2, [k1, p1] 11 times, p1, k3; rep from * across, end last repeat k10.
Row 5: K11, *yo, [k1, p1] 11 times, k1, yo, k5; rep from * across, end last repeat k11—137 sts.
Row 6: K11, *p2, [k1, p1] 11 times, p1, k5; rep from * across, end last repeat k11.
Row 7: K12, *yo, [k1, p1] 11 times, k1, yo, k7; rep from * across, end last repeat k12—145 sts.
Row 8: K12, p2, [k1, p1] 11 times, p1, k7; rep from * across, end last repeat k12.
Row 9: K13, *yo, [k1, p1] 11 times, k1, yo, k9; rep from * across, end last repeat k13—153 sts.
Row 10: K13, *p2, [k1, p1] 11 times, p1, k9; rep from * across, end last repeat k13.
Row 11: K14, *yo, [k1, p1] 11 times, k1, yo, k11; rep from * across, end last repeat k14—161 sts.
Row 12: K14, *p2, [k1, p1] 11 times, p1, k11; rep from * across, end last repeat k14.
Row 13: K15, *[ssk] 5 times, sl 1—k2tog—psso, [k2tog] 5 times, k13; rep from * across, end last repeat k15—113 sts.
Row 14: K8, [k1, p1] until 9 sts rem, k9.
Cont working Rows 1–14 until blanket meas approx 26½", ending after Row 13 of Fan Pattern.

Begin garter stitch edge
Next row: (WS) Knit.
Cont in garter st for 12 more rows, ending after a WS row.
Next row: (RS) BO all sts knitwise.

Finishing
Weave in ends. Steam or wet block pc to measurements.

Key

- ☐ knit on RS, purl on WS
- ⊟ purl on RS, knit on WS
- ⊡ yo
- ⊠ ssk
- ⅄ sl—k2tog—psso
- ⊿ k2tog
- ⬛ no stitch
- ⬜ pattern repeat

Fan Pattern

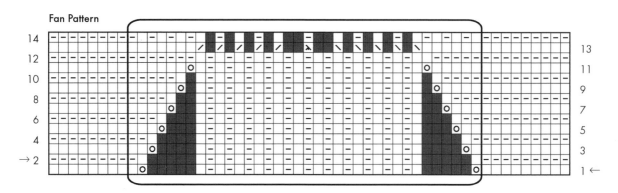

sibella cardigan

Finished Bust Measurements
31 (35, 39, 43, 47, 51, 55¼)"
Shown in size 35"

Yarn
Canopy Fingering by The Fibre Co.
(50% baby alpaca, 30% merino wool, 20% viscose
from bamboo; 200yds [183m]/50g)
• 6 (6, 7, 7, 8, 9, 9) skeins in Manatee
OR 1040 (1135, 1230, 1400, 1500, 1645,
1765) yds fingering weight yarn

Needles
• One 32" circular needle (circ) in size US 4
  [3.5 mm]
• One pair straight needles in size US 4 [3.5 mm]
Or size needed to obtain gauge

Notions
• Stitch markers
• Waste yarn
• Tapestry needle for weaving in ends
• Nine ½" buttons

Gauge
24 sts and 34 rows = 4" in St st, blocked.
14 rows = 1½" in Flower Pattern.

Flower Pattern (multiple of 22 sts + 2)
(Also, see chart page 64)
Row 1: (WS) Knit.
Rows 2–3: Knit.
Row 4: (RS) K1, *p2, yo, k4, ssk, k6, k2tog, k4, yo,
p2; rep from * to last st, k1.
Row 5: P1, *k3, yo, p4, p2tog, p4, p2tog-tbl, p4,
yo, k3; rep from * to last st, p1.
Row 6: K1, *p4, yo, k4, ssk, k2, k2tog, k4, yo, p4;
rep from * to last st, k1.
Row 7: P1, *k5, yo, p4, p2tog, p2tog-tbl, p4, yo,
k5; rep from * to last st, p1.
Rows 8–11: Rep Rows 4–7 one time.
Row 12: K1, purl to last st, k1.

Row 13: Purl.
Row 14: Rep Row 12.
Work Rows 1–14 for Flower Pattern.

Note
Cardigan is worked from the bottom up in one piece.
Sleeves are worked flat and joined to body at yoke.
Yoke is shaped with round yoke shaping.

Cardigan
Body
With circ and using the long-tail cast on, CO 184
(208, 232, 256, 280, 304, 328) sts. Do not join.

Begin 2x2 rib
First row: (WS) P1, *p2, k2; rep from * to last 3
sts, p3.
Next row: (RS) K1, *k2, p2; rep from * to last 3
sts, k3.
Cont in rib as est until pc meas 2½" from beg, ending
after a RS row.

Next row: (WS) Knit.
Knit 2 more rows.

Begin stockinette stitch
Next row *dec row and place markers:* (RS) K45 (51, 57, 63, 69, 75, 81), place marker (pm), k1, k2tog, k88 (100, 112, 124, 136, 148, 160), ssk, k1, pm, knit to end—182 (206, 230, 254, 278, 302, 326) sts.
Next row: (WS) Purl to end, slipping markers.
Cont in St st until pc meas 5½" from beg.

Begin side shaping
Next row *dec row:* *Knit to 3 sts before m, ssk, k1, sl m, k1, k2tog; rep from * one more time, knit to end (4 sts dec'd)—178 (202, 226, 250, 274, 298, 322) sts.
Cont in St st and rep *dec row* every 12th row 2 more times—170 (194, 218, 242, 266, 290, 314) sts.

Cont in St st until pc meas 9½" from beg.

Next row *inc row:* *Knit to 1 st before m, m1-R, k1, sl m, k1, m1-L; rep from * one more time (4 sts inc'd)—174 (198, 222, 246, 270, 294, 318) sts.
Rep *inc row* every 10th row one time, then every 12th row one time—182 (206, 230, 254, 278, 302, 326) sts.

Cont in St st until pc meas 14½" from beg, ending after a RS row.

Bind-off for armholes
Next row: (WS) *Purl to 4 (5, 6, 6, 7, 9, 10) sts before side m, BO 8 (10, 12, 12, 14, 18, 20) sts, removing m; rep from * one more time, purl to end—41 (46, 51, 57, 62, 66, 71) sts each front; 84 (94, 104, 116, 126, 134, 144) sts for back.
Keep sts on circ. Do not break yarn. Set aside.

Sleeves
With straight needles and using the long-tail cast on, CO 46 (46, 50, 54, 54, 58, 62) sts.

Begin 2x2 rib cuff
First row: (WS) P1, *k2, p2; rep from * to last st, p1.
Next row: (RS) K1, *k2, p2; rep from * to last st, k1.
Cont in rib as est until sleeve meas 2" from beg, ending after a RS row.

Next row: (WS) Knit.

Knit 2 more rows.

Sizes 31 (-, 39, 43, -, 51, -)" only:
Next row *dec row:* (RS) K2tog, knit to end—45 (-, 49, 53, -, 57, -) sts.
Next row: Purl.

All Sizes:
Begin stockinette stitch
Next row: (RS) Knit.
Next row: Purl.
Cont in St st until sleeve meas 4" from beg, ending after a WS row.

Begin sleeve shaping
Next row *inc row:* (RS) K2, m1-R, knit to last 2 sts, m1-L, k2 (2 sts inc'd)—47 (48, 51, 55, 56, 59, 64) sts.
Rep *inc row* every 8 (8, 8, 6, 6, 6, 6)th row 12 (13, 13, 16, 17, 19, 18) more times—71 (74, 77, 87, 90, 97, 100) sts.
Cont in St st until sleeve meas 18" from beg, ending after a WS row.

Begin underarm shaping
BO 5 (6, 7, 7, 8, 10, 11) sts at beg of next 2 rows—61 (62, 63, 73, 74, 77, 78) sts.
Slip sts to waste yarn; break yarn. Set aside.

Repeat for second sleeve.

Yoke
Join sleeve stitches to body
Next row: (RS) K41 (46, 51, 57, 62, 66, 71) right front sts, transfer 61 (62, 63, 73, 74, 77, 78) held sleeve sts to needle with RS facing and knit across, k84 (94, 104, 116, 126, 134, 144) back sts, transfer 61 (62, 63, 73, 74, 77, 78) held sleeve sts to needle with RS facing and knit across, k41 (46, 51, 57, 62, 66, 71) left front sts—288 (310, 332, 376, 398, 420, 442) sts on needle.

Work 4 (6, 6, 12, 16, 22, 26) rows in St st, ending after a RS row.

Begin first Flower Pattern section
Row 1: (WS) Work Row 1 of Flower Pattern.
Cont working Rows 2–14 of Flower Pattern.
Next row: (WS) Purl.

Begin first row of yoke shaping

Next row *dec row:* (RS) K1, *[k3, k2tog] 4 (5, 3, 5, 3, 4, 5) times, [k1, k2tog] 2 (1, 5, 3, 7, 6, 5) time(s); rep from * to last st, k1 (66 [66, 88, 88, 110, 110, 110] sts dec'd)—222 (244, 244, 288, 288, 310, 332) sts.

Next row: (WS) Purl.
Next row: (RS) Knit.

Begin second Flower Pattern section

Work Rows 1–14 of Flower Pattern.
Next row: (WS) Purl.

Begin second row of yoke shaping

Next row *dec row:* (RS) K1, *[k2, k2tog] 4 (5, 5, 5, 5, 6, 5) times, [k2tog] 2 (1, 1, 3, 3, 2, 5) time(s); rep from * to last st, k1 (66 [66, 66, 88, 88, 88, 110] sts dec'd)—156 (178, 178, 200, 200, 222, 222) sts.
Next row: (WS) Purl.
Next row: (RS) Knit.

Begin third Flower Pattern section

Work Rows 1–13 of Flower Pattern.

Begin third row of yoke shaping

Next row *dec row:* (RS) K1, *[p2tog, p1] 3 (2, 2, 3, 3, 3, 3) times, p2tog; rep from * to last st, k1 (56 [66, 66, 72, 72, 80, 80] sts dec'd)—100 (112, 112, 128, 128, 142, 142) sts rem.

Sizes 31 (35, 39, 43, 47, -, -)" only:
Begin 2x2 rib neckband

Next row: (WS) P1, *p2, k2; rep from * to last st, p3.
Next row: (RS) K1, *k2, p2; rep from * to last st, k3.

Sizes - (-, -, -, -, 51, 55)" only:
Begin 2 x 2 rib neckband

Next row: (WS) P2, *p2, k2; rep from * to last 4 sts, p4.
Next row: (RS) K2, *k2, p2; rep from * to last 4 sts, k4.

All Sizes:

Cont as est until rib meas ½", ending after a WS row.
Next row: (RS) BO all sts in pattern.

Finishing

Weave in ends. Block to measurements. Sew sleeves and underarms.

Buttonband

With RS facing and beg at top edge of left front neckband, pick up and knit 115 (117, 117, 121, 123, 127, 131) sts.
First row: (WS) Knit.
Knit 5 more rows.

Next row: (WS) Loosely BO all sts knitwise.

Buttonhole band

With RS facing and beg at the bottom of right front hem, pick up and knit 115 (117, 117, 121, 123, 127, 131) sts.
First row: (WS) Knit.
Knit 2 more rows.
Next row *buttonhole row:* (RS) K4 (6, 6, 8, 9, 7, 5), *yo, k2tog, k11 (11, 11, 11, 11, 12, 13); rep from * for a total of 8 times, then yo, k2tog, k5 (5, 5, 7, 8, 6, 4) sts to end.
Knit 2 more rows.

Next row: (WS) Loosely BO all sts knitwise.

Sew buttons onto buttonband opposite buttonholes. Weave in loose ends.

Key

☐ knit on RS, purl on WS

⊟ purl on RS, knit on WS

⊡ yo

⬂ ssk on RS, p2tog-tbl on WS

⬀ k2tog on RS, p2tog on WS

⬛ pattern repeat

Flower Pattern chart

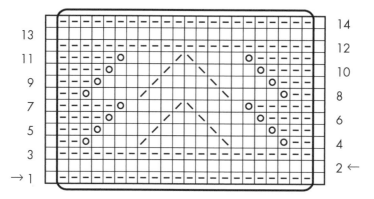

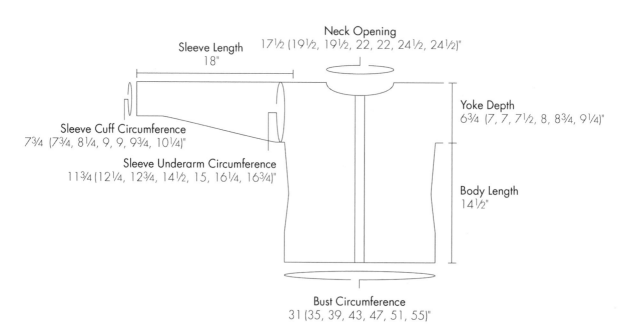

Sleeve Length
18"

Neck Opening
17½ (19½, 19½, 22, 22, 24½, 24½)"

Yoke Depth
6¾ (7, 7, 7½, 8, 8¾, 9¼)"

Sleeve Cuff Circumference
7¾ (7¾, 8¼, 9, 9, 9¾, 10¼)"

Sleeve Underarm Circumference
11¾ (12¼, 12¾, 14½, 15, 16¼, 16¾)"

Body Length
14½"

Bust Circumference
31 (35, 39, 43, 47, 51, 55)"

sibella cowl

Finished Measurements
58¾" in circumference, 7" high

Yarn
Tern by Quince & Co.
(75% American wool, 25% silk; 221yds
[202m]/50g)
• 3 skeins in Mist
OR 550 yds fingering weight yarn

Needles
• One 32" circular needle (circ) in size US 4
  [3.5 mm]
Or size needed to obtain gauge

Notions
• Tapestry needle for weaving in ends

Gauge
26 sts and 39 rnds = 4" in Flower Pattern, blocked.

Note
Cowl is worked in the round.

Flower Pattern (multiple of 20 sts + 2)
(Also, see chart below)
Rnd 1: Purl.
Rnd 2: Knit.
Rnd 3: Purl.
Rnd 4: *P2, yo, k4, ssk, k6, k2tog, k4, yo; rep
from * to last 2 sts, p2.
Rnd 5: *P3, yo, k4, ssk, k4, k2tog, k4, yo, p1; rep
from * to last 2 sts, p2.
Rnd 6: *P4, yo, k4, ssk, k2, k2tog, k4, yo, p2; rep
from * to to last 2 sts, p2.
Rnd 7: *P5, yo, k4, ssk, k2tog, k4, yo, p3; rep
from * to to last 2 sts, p2.
Rnds 8–11: Rep Rnds 4–7 one time.
Rnd 12: Purl.
Rnd 13: Knit.
Rnd 14: Purl.
Rnds 15–18: Knit.

Key
☐ knit
⊟ purl
⊡ yo
⧹ ssk
⧸ k2tog
☐ pattern repeat

Cowl
Using the long-tail cast on, CO 382 sts. Place
marker (pm) for BOR and join to work in the rnd,
being careful not to twist sts.

Begin Flower Pattern
First rnd: Work all sts in Rnd 1 of Flower Pattern.
Cont working Rnds 2–18 of Flower Pattern one time,
then Rnds 1–18 two times, then Rnds 1–14 one
time; cowl meas approx 7" from beg.

Next rnd: BO all sts knitwise.

Finishing
Weave in ends. Wet block pc to measurements.

Flower Pattern chart

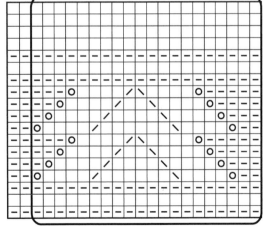

sibella pullover

Finished Bust Measurements
30 (34, 38, 42, 46, 50, 54)"
Shown in size 34"

Yarn
Road to China Light by The Fibre Co. (65% baby alpaca, 15% silk, 10% camel, 10% cashmere; 159 yds [145 m] /50 g)
• 6 (6, 7, 8, 8, 9, 10) skeins in Grey Pearl
OR
955 (1045, 1160, 1300, 1420, 1560, 1685) yds sport weight yarn

Needles
• One 24" and 32" circular needle (circ) in size US 5 [3.75 mm]
• One 16" circ in size US 4 [3.5 mm]
• One set dpns in sizes US 4 and 5 [3.5 and 3.75 mm]
Or size needed to obtain gauge

Notions
• Stitch markers
• Waste yarn
• Tapestry needle for weaving in ends

Gauge
24 sts and 34 rnds = 4" in St st with larger needle, blocked.
14 rnds = 1½" in Flower Pattern with larger needles.

Flower pattern (multiple of 22 sts)
(Also, see chart page 68)
Rnd 1: Purl.
Rnd 2: Knit.
Rnd 3: Purl.
Rnd 4: *P2, yo, k4, ssk, k6, k2tog, k4, yo, p2; rep from * to end.
Rnd 5: *P3, yo, k4, ssk, k4, k2rog, k4, yo, p3; rep from * to end.
Rnd 6: *P4, yo, k4, ssk, k2, k2tog, k4, yo, p4; rep from * to end.
Rnd 7: *P5, yo, k4, ssk, k2tog, k4, yo, p5; rep from * to end.
Rnds 8–11: Rep Rnds 4–7 one time.
Rnd 12: Purl.
Rnd 13: Knit.
Rnd 14: Purl.

Note
Pullover is worked from the bottom up in one piece. Sleeves are worked in the round and joined at yoke. Yoke is shaped with round yoke shaping.

Pullover
Body
With longer, larger circ and using the long-tail cast on, CO 180 (204, 228, 252, 276, 300, 324) sts. Place marker (pm) for BOR and join to work in the rnd, being careful not to twist sts.

Begin 2x2 rib
First rnd: *K2, p2; rep from * to end.
Cont to work rib as est until pc meas 2½" from beg.

Begin garter stitch
First rnd: Purl.
Next rnd: Knit.
Next rnd: Purl.

Begin stockinette stitch
Next rnd *place marker:* K90 (102, 114, 126, 138, 150, 162) sts, pm for side, knit to end.
Cont in St st until body meas 5" from beg.

Begin side shaping

Next rnd *dec rnd:* *K1, k2tog, work to 3 sts before side m, ssk, k1, sl m; rep from * one time—(4 sts dec'd) 176 (200, 224, 248, 272, 296, 320) sts. Rep *dec rnd* every 12th rnd two more times—168 (192, 216, 240, 264, 288, 312) sts.

Cont in St st until body meas 9" from beg.

Next rnd *inc rnd:* [K1, m1-L, work to 1 st before side m, m1-R, k1, sl m] two times—(4 sts inc'd) 172 (196, 220, 244, 468, 292, 316) sts. Rep *inc rnd* every 10th rnd one time, then every 12th rnd one time—180 (204, 228, 252, 276, 300, 324) sts.

Cont in St st until body meas approx 13" from beg.

Begin underarm bind-off

Next rnd: Knit to last 4 (5, 6, 6, 7, 9, 10) sts, BO 8 (10, 12, 12, 14, 18, 20) sts, removing BOR m.
Next rnd: Knit to 4 (5, 6, 6, 7, 9, 10) sts before side marker, BO 8 (10, 12, 12, 14, 18, 20) sts, removing side marker, knit to end—82 (92, 102, 114, 124, 132, 142) sts rem for each front and back. Do not break yarn. Set aside.

Sleeves

With smaller dpns and using the long-tail cast on, CO 60 (60, 64, 64, 68, 72, 76) sts. Divide sts evenly onto four needles, pm for BOR and join to work in the rnd, being careful not to twist sts.

Begin 2x2 rib cuff

First rnd: *K2, p2; rep from * to end.
Cont to work rib as est until pc meas 2" from beg.

Begin garter stitch

First rnd: Purl.
Next rnd: Knit.
Next rnd: Purl.

Change to larger dpns.

Begin stockinette stitch

Next rnd: Knit, and at the same time, dec 1 (dec 0, dec 3, inc 1, dec 2, inc 1, dec 2) st(s) evenly around—59 (60, 61, 65, 66, 73, 74) sts.

Begin sleeve shaping

Next rnd *inc rnd:* K2, m1-R, knit to last 2 sts, m1-L, k2—(2 sts inc'd) 61 (62, 63, 67, 68, 75, 76) sts. Rep *inc rnd* every 12 (10, 10, 6, 6, 6, 6)th rnd 1 (1, 3, 5, 4, 4, 8) time(s), every 14 (12, 12, 8, 8, 8, 8)th rnd 1 (1, 2, 3, 4, 4, 2) time(s), then every 16 (14, 14, 10, 10, 10, 10)th rnd 2 (3, 1, 2, 1, 1, 1) time(s)—69 (72, 75, 85, 88, 95, 98) sts. Cont in St st until sleeve meas 12" from beg.

Begin underarm shaping

Next rnd: Knit to last 4 (5, 6, 6, 7, 9, 10) sts, BO 8 (10, 12, 12, 14, 18, 20) sts—61 (62, 63, 73, 74, 77, 78) sts rem.
Next rnd: Knit to end.
Slip sts to waste yarn; break yarn. Set aside.

Yoke
Join sleeve sts to body

Note: Change to shorter circ when necessary.
Next rnd: Pm for BOR, k61 (62, 63, 73, 74, 77, 78) sleeve sts to yoke, k82 (92, 102, 114, 124, 132, 142) front sts, k61 (62, 63, 73, 74, 77, 78) sleeve sts to yoke, k82 (92, 102, 114, 124, 132, 142) back sts to end—286 (308, 330, 374, 396, 418, 440) sts total.

Knit 0 (1, 5, 11, 16, 21, 26) rnd(s).

Begin first Flower Pattern section

Work Rnds 1–14 across all sts for Flower Pattern.
Next rnd: Knit.

Begin first round of yoke shaping

Next rnd *dec rnd:* *[K3, k2tog] 4 (5, 3, 5, 3, 4, 5) times, [k1, k2og] 2 (1, 5, 3, 7, 6, 5) time(s); rep from * to end (66 (66, 88, 88, 110, 110, 110) sts dec'd)—220 (242, 242, 286, 286, 308, 330) sts.
Next rnd: Knit.

Begin second Flower Pattern section

Work Rnds 1–14 across all sts for Flower Pattern.
Next rnd: Knit.

Begin second round of yoke shaping

Next rnd *dec rnd:* *[K2, k2tog] 4 (5, 5, 5, 5, 6, 5) times, [k2tog] 2 (1, 1, 3, 3, 2, 5) time(s); rep from * to end (66 (66, 66, 88, 88, 88, 110) sts dec'd)—154 (176, 176, 198, 198, 220, 220) sts.

Next rnd: Knit.

Begin third Flower Pattern section

Work Rnds 1–13 across all sts for Flower Pattern.

Begin third round of yoke shaping

Size 30 (-, -, -, -, -, -)" only:

Next rnd *dec rnd:* P2tog, *[p2tog, p1] 2 times, p2tog; rep from * to end (58 sts dec'd)—96 (-, -, -, -, -, -) sts.

Sizes - (34, 38, -, -, -, -)" only:

Next rnd *dec rnd:* P2tog, p3, *[p2tog, p1] 2 times, p2tog; rep from * to last 3 sts, p3 (64 sts dec'd)— - (112, 112, -, -, -, -) sts.

Flower Pattern chart

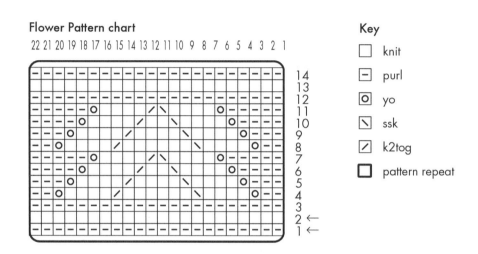

Key

☐	knit
⊟	purl
⊙	yo
◳	ssk
◰	k2tog
☐	pattern repeat

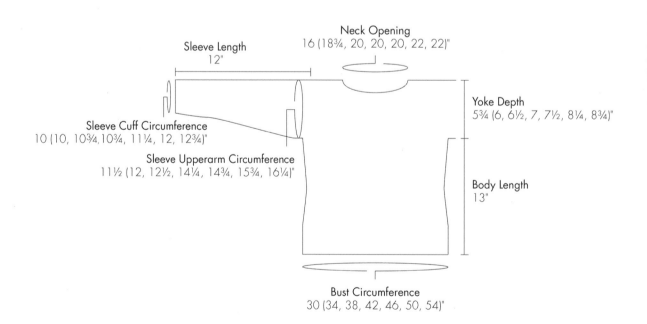

Neck Opening
16 (18¾, 20, 20, 20, 22, 22)"

Sleeve Length
12"

Yoke Depth
5¾ (6, 6½, 7, 7½, 8¼, 8¾)"

Sleeve Cuff Circumference
10 (10, 10¾, 10¾, 11¼, 12, 12¾)"

Sleeve Upperarm Circumference
11½ (12, 12½, 14¼, 14¾, 15¾, 16¼)"

Body Length
13"

Bust Circumference
30 (34, 38, 42, 46, 50, 54)"

Sizes - (-, -, 42, 46, -, -)" only:
Next rnd *dec rnd:* P2tog, p2, *[p2tog, p1] 2 times, p2tog; rep from * to last 4 sts, p2tog, p2 (78 sts dec'd)— - (-, -,120, 120, -, -) sts.

Sizes - (-, -, -, -, 50, 54)" only:
Next rnd *dec rnd:* *[p2tog, p1] 2 times, p2tog; rep from * to end (88 sts dec'd)— - (-, -, -, -, 132, 132) sts.

All Sizes:
Yoke meas approx 5¼ (5½, 6, 6½, 7, 7¾, 8¼)" from underarm.

Change to smaller needles.

Begin 2x2 rib neckband
First rnd: *K2, p2; rep from * to end.
Cont in rib as est until rib meas ½" from beg of rib.

Next rnd: BO all sts in patt.

Finishing
Sew underarm seams. Weave in ends. Steam or wet block pc to measurements.

---

sibella scarf

Finished Measurements
10½" wide, 83" long
Yarn
Tern by Quince & Co.
(75% American wool, 25% silk); 221yds [202m]/50g
• 4 skeins in Oyster *(Sample took 4 entire skeins)*
OR 880 yds fingering weight yarn
Needles
• One pair straight needles in size US 4 [3.5 mm]
Or size needed to obtain gauge
Notions
• Waste yarn
• Tapestry needle for weaving in ends
Gauge
26 sts and 34 rows = 4" in St st, blocked.

Note
Scarf is worked in 2 pieces and grafted together.

Scarf
First panel (make 2)
Using the long-tail cast on, CO 68 sts.

Begin scarf pattern
Row 1: (WS) Knit.
Row 2: Knit.
Row 3: Knit.
Row 4: K3 (edge sts, keep in garter st), *p2, yo, k4, ssk, k6, k2tog, k4, yo; rep from * to last 5 sts, p2, k3 (edge sts, keep in garter st).
Row 5: K3, *k3, yo, p4, p2tog, p4, p2tog-tbl, p4, yo, k1; rep from * to last 5 sts, k5.

Row 6: K3, *p4, yo, k4, ssk, k2, k2tog, k4, yo, p2; rep from * to last 5 sts, p2, k3.
Row 7: K3, *k5, yo, p4, p2tog, p2tog-tbl, p4, yo, k3; rep from * to last 5 sts, k5.
Rows 8–11: Rep Rows 4–7 one time.
Row 12: K3, purl to last 3 sts, k3.
Row 13: K3, purl to last 3 sts, k3.
Row 14: K3, purl to last 3 sts, k3.
Row 15: K3, purl to last 3 sts, k3.
Row 16: Knit.
Row 17: K3, purl to last 3 sts, k3.
Rows 18–23: Rep Rows 16–17 three more times.
Row 24: Knit.
Rep Rows 1–24 for scarf pattern until pc meas approx 41½" from beg, ending after Row 18. Thread with waste yarn and set aside.

Make the second scarf panel same as the first. Graft ends of the two panels together.

Finishing
Weave in ends. Wet block pc to measurements.

IMOGEN

imogen tee

Finished Bust Measurements
32½ (35¾, 39, 42½, 45¾, 49, 52½)"
Shown in size 35¾"

Yarn
Tern by Quince & Co. (75% American wool, 25% silk; 221yds [202m]/50g)
• 4 (4, 5, 5, 6, 6, 7) skeins Terra Cotta
OR 760 (825, 895, 1095, 1170, 1245, 1315) yds fingering weight yarn

Needles
• One 16" and 29" circular needle (circ) in size US 5 [3.75 mm]
• One set of dpns in size US 5 [3.75 mm]
Or size needed to obtain gauge

Notions
• Stitch markers in 2 different colors
• Waste yarn
• Tapestry needle for weaving in ends

Gauge
24 sts and 32 rnds = 4" in St st, blocked.

Frost Flowers (panel of 36 sts)
(Also, see chart page 72)
Rnd 1: K1, yo, ssk, k2, yo, ssk, p2, yo, k4, ssk, k6, k2tog, k4, yo, p2, k2, yo, ssk, k3.
Rnd 2: P1, k2, k2tog, yo, k2, p2, k1, yo, k4, ssk, k4, k2tog, k4, yo, k1, p2, k2tog, yo, k2, k2tog, yo, p1.
Rnd 3: K1, yo, ssk, k2, yo, ssk, p2, k2, yo, k4, ssk, k2, k2tog, k4, yo, k2, p2, k2, yo, ssk, k3.
Rnd 4: P1, k2, k2tog, yo, k2, p2, k3, yo, k4, ssk, k2tog, k4, yo, k3, p2, k2tog, yo, k2, k2tog, yo, p1.
Rnds 5–12: Rep Rows 1–4 two more times.
Rnd 13: K4, k2tog, k4, yo, p2, [k2, yo, ssk] three times, p2, yo, k4, ssk, k4.
Rnd 14: P1, k2, k2tog, k4, yo, k1, p2, [k2tog, yo, k2] three times, p2, k1, yo, k4, ssk, k2, p1.
Rnd 15: K2, k2tog, k4, yo, k2, p2, [k2, yo, ssk] three times, p2, k2, yo, k4, ssk, k2.

Rnd 16: P1, k2tog, k4, yo, k3, p2, [k2tog, yo, k2] three times, p2, k3, yo, k4, ssk, p1.
Rnds 17–24: Rep Rnds 13–16 two more times.
Rep Rnds 1–24 for Frost Flowers.

Note
Tee is worked from the bottom up with raglan shaping.

Tee
Body
With longer circ and using the long-tail cast on, CO 196 (216, 236, 256, 276, 296, 316) sts, place marker (pm) for BOR and join to work in the rnd, being careful not to twist sts.

Begin garter stitch
Rnd 1: Purl.
Rnd 2: Knit.
Rep Rnds 1 and 2 two more times.

Begin Frost Flowers and stockinette stitch
Next rnd *place markers:* K31 (36, 41, 46, 51, 56, 61), pm for Frost Flowers, work 36 sts in Rnd 1 of Frost Flowers, pm for Frost Flowers, k31 (36, 41, 46, 51, 56, 61), pm for side, k to end.
Work as est for 22 (22, 22, 44, 44, 40, 38) more rnds; pc meas approx 3½ (3½, 3½, 6¼, 6¼, 6¼, 5¾, 5½)" from beg.

Begin side shaping
Next rnd *dec rnd:* K1, k2tog, work to 3 sts before side m, ssk, k1, sl m, k1, k2tog, work to last 3 sts, ssk, k1 (4 sts dec'd)—192 (212, 232, 252, 272, 292, 312) sts.
Rep *dec rnd* every 14th rnd two more times—184 (204, 224, 244, 264, 284, 304) sts.

Cont to work as est for 14 more rnds; pc meas approx 9 (9, 9, 11¾, 11¾, 11¼, 11)" from beg.

Next rnd *inc rnd:* K1, m1-L, work to 1 st before side m, m1-R, k1, sl m, k1, m1-L, work to last st, m1-R, k1(4 sts inc'd)—188 (208, 228, 248, 268, 288, 308) sts.
Rep *inc rnd* every 12th rnd 2 (2, 1, 1, 0, 0, 0) more time(s), then every 10th rnd 0 (0, 1, 1, 1, 1, 0) time(s), then every 8th rnd 0 (0, 0, 0, 1, 1, 2) time(s)—196 (216, 236, 256, 276, 296, 316) sts.

Cont to work as est for 11 (9, 7, 5, 5, 5, 5) more rnds, ending on Rnd 6 (4, 24, 20, 16, 12, 8) of Frost Flowers; 102 (100, 96, 116, 112, 108, 104) rnds in Frost Flowers worked to here; pc meas approx 13½ (13¼, 12¾, 15¼, 14¾, 14¼, 13¾)" from beg.

Begin underarm bind-off
Next rnd: Work as est to last 5 (5, 6, 6, 7, 7, 8) sts, BO 10 (10, 12, 12, 14, 14, 16) sts, removing BOR marker.
Next rnd: Work as est to 5 (5, 6, 6, 7, 7, 8) sts before side marker, BO 10 (10, 12, 12, 14, 14, 16) sts, removing side marker, knit to end—88 (98, 106, 116, 124, 134, 142) sts rem on each side; 104 (102, 98, 118, 114, 110, 106) rnds in Frost Flowers worked to here. Set aside.

Sleeves
With dpns and using the long-tail cast on, CO 66 (69, 77, 83, 89, 95, 101) sts. Pm for BOR and join to work in the rnd, being careful not to twist sts.

Begin garter stitch cuff
Rnd 1: Purl.
Rnd 2: Knit.
Rep Rnds 1 and 2 two more times.

Begin underarm bind-off
Next rnd: Knit to last 5 (5, 6, 6, 7, 7, 8) sts, BO 10 (10, 12, 12, 14, 14, 16) sts.
Next rnd: Knit to end.
Slip sts to waste yarn; break yarn. Set aside.
Repeat for second sleeve.

Yoke
Join sleeve sts to body
Next rnd *place raglan markers:* Transfer 56 (59, 65, 71, 75, 81, 85) sleeve sts to longer needle, pm for BOR, k56 (59, 65, 71, 75, 81, 85) sleeve sts to yoke, pm, work as est across 88 (98, 106, 116, 124, 134, 142) front sts, pm, transfer 56 (59, 65, 71, 75, 81, 85) sleeve sts to needle, k56 (59, 65, 71, 75, 81, 85) sleeve sts to yoke, pm, k88 (98, 106, 116, 124, 134, 142) sts across back—288 (314, 342, 374, 398, 430, 454) sts total.

As you proceed with the yoke, continue working Frost Flowers between markers as est, all other stitches are worked in St st.
Work 3 (3, 2, 2, 2, 2, 2) rnds even.

Begin raglan shaping
For Sizes 32¾ and 35¾":
Skip to All sizes below.

For Sizes - (-, 39¼ , 42¾, 46, 49¼, 52¾)":
Next rnd *body only dec rnd:* *Work as est to raglan m, sl m, k1, k2tog, work to 3 sts before next raglan m, ssk, k1, sl m; rep from * one more time (4 sts dec'd)— - (-, 338, 370, 394, 426, 450).
Rep *body only dec rnd* every rnd - (-, 0, 1, 2, 4, 5) more time(s)— - (-, 338, 366, 386, 410, 430) sts remain.

All sizes:
Next rnd *dec rnd:* *K1, k2tog, work to 3 sts before next raglan marker, ssk, k1, sl m; rep from * 3 times

71

(8 sts dec'd)—280 (306, 330, 358, 378, 402, 422) sts rem.

Rep *dec rnd* every rnd 0 (0, 0, 3, 4, 8, 9) time(s), then every 4th rnd 3 (1, 0, 0, 0, 0, 0) time(s), then every other row 17 (22, 26, 26, 27, 26, 27) times—120 (122, 122, 126, 130, 130, 134) sts rem [46 (50, 50, 52, 54, 54, 56) sts for front and back, 14 (11, 11, 11, 11, 11, 11) sts for each sleeve].

Work 1 rnd even, this will be Rnd 12 of Frost Flowers.

Begin garter stitch

Next rnd: Purl.
Next rnd: Knit.
Rep Rnds last 2 rnds one more time.

Next rnd: Purl.
Next rnd: BO all sts knitwise.

Finishing

Weave in ends. Sew underarm seams. Steam block to measurements.

Frost Flowers

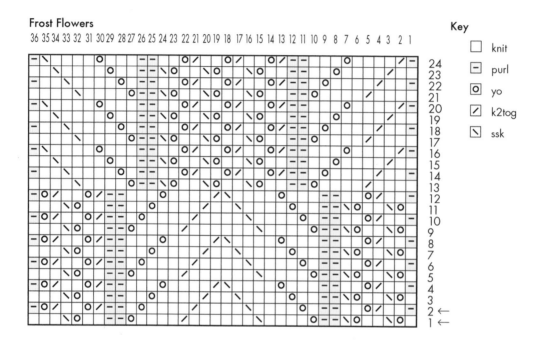

Key

- ☐ knit
- ⊟ purl
- ☉ yo
- ⟋ k2tog
- ⟍ ssk

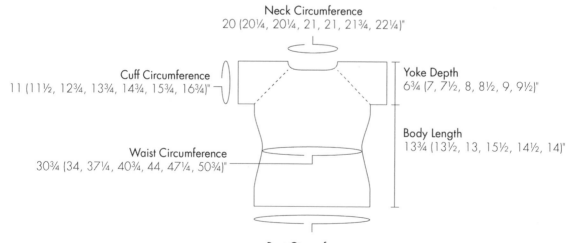

Neck Circumference
20 (20¼, 20¼, 21, 21, 21¾, 22¼)"

Cuff Circumference
11 (11½, 12¾, 13¾, 14¾, 15¾, 16¾)"

Yoke Depth
6¾ (7, 7½, 8, 8½, 9, 9½)"

Body Length
13¾ (13½, 13, 15½, 14½, 14)"

Waist Circumference
30¾ (34, 37¼, 40¾, 44, 47¼, 50¾)"

Bust Circumference
32½ (35¾, 39, 42½, 45¾, 49, 52½)"

imogen
spring

imogen
wool

imogen spring & wool

Finished Bust Measurements
32¾ (34, 36, 38, 39¼, 42¾, 46, 49¼, 52¾)"
Shown in size 34"

Yarn
For Imogen Spring: Canopy Fingering by The Fibre Co.
(50% baby alpaca, 30% merino wool, 20% viscose from bamboo; 200yds [183m]/50g)
• 5 (5, 5, 5, 5, 5, 6, 6, 6) skeins; shown in Cloud Forest

For Imogen Wool: Finch by Quince & Co.
(100% American wool; 221yds [202m]/50g)
• 6 (6, 6, 6, 7, 8, 8, 8, 9) skeins Chanterelle
OR
For Imogen Spring: 840 (865, 890, 915, 950, 1000, 1050, 1110, 1160) yds
For Imogen Wool: 1220 (1255, 1275, 1290, 1345, 1420, 1495, 1565, 1640) yds fingering weight yarn

Needles
• One 16" and 29" circular needle (circ) in size US 5 [3.75 mm]
• One set of dpns in size US 5 [3.75 mm]
Or size needed to obtain gauge

Notions
• Stitch markers in 2 different colors
• Waste yarn
• Tapestry needle for weaving in ends

Gauge
24 sts and 32 rnds = 4" in St st, blocked.

Frost Flowers (panel of 36 sts)
(Also, see chart page 72)
Rnd 1: K1, yo, ssk, k2, yo, ssk, p2, yo, k4, ssk, k6, k2tog, k4, yo, p2, k2, yo, ssk, k3.

Rnd 2: P1, k2, k2tog, yo, k2, p2, k1, yo, k4, ssk, k4, k2tog, k4, yo, k1, p2, k2tog, yo, k2, k2tog, yo, p1.
Rnd 3: K1, yo, ssk, k2, yo, ssk, p2, k2, yo, k4, ssk, k2, k2tog, k4, yo, k2, p2, k2, yo, ssk, k3.
Rnd 4: P1, k2, k2tog, yo, k2, p2, k3, yo, k4, ssk, k2tog, k4, yo, k3, p2, k2tog, yo, k2, k2tog, yo, p1.
Rnds 5–12: Rep Rows 1–4 two more times.
Rnd 13: K4, k2tog, k4, yo, p2, [k2, yo, ssk] three times, p2, yo, k4, ssk, k4.
Rnd 14: P1, k2, k2tog, k4, yo, k1, p2, [k2tog, yo, k2] three times, p2, k1, yo, k4, ssk, k2, p1.
Rnd 15: K2, k2tog, k4, yo, k2, p2, [k2, yo, ssk] three times, p2, k2, yo, k4, ssk, k2.
Rnd 16: P1, k2tog, k4, yo, k3, p2, [k2tog, yo, k2] three times, p2, k3, yo, k4, ssk, p1.
Rnds 17–24: Rep Rnds 13–16 two more times.
Rep Rnds 1–24 for Frost Flowers.

Note
Tee is worked from the bottom up with raglan shaping.

Pullover
Body
Using the long-tail cast on, CO 196 (204, 216, 228, 236, 256, 276, 296, 316) sts. Place marker (pm) for BOR and join to work in the rnd, being careful not to twist sts.

Begin garter stitch
First rnd: Purl.
Next rnd: Knit.
Work last 2 rnds two more times.

Begin Frost Flowers and stockinette stitch

Next rnd *place markers:* K31 (33, 36, 39, 41, 46, 51, 56, 61), pm for Frost Flowers, work 36 sts in Rnd 1 of Frost Flowers, pm for Frost Flowers, k31 (33 , 36, 39, 41, 46, 51, 56, 61), pm for side, knit to end.

Work as est for 22 (22, 22, 22, 44, 44, 44, 40, 38) more rnds; pc meas approx 3½ (3½, 3½, 6¼, 6¼, 6¼, 5¾, 5½)" from beg.

Begin side shaping

Next rnd *dec rnd:* K1, k2tog, work to 3 sts before side m, ssk, k1, sl m, k1, k2tog, work to last 3 sts, ssk, k1 (4 sts dec'd)—192 (200, 212, 224, 232, 252, 272, 292, 312) sts.
Rep *dec rnd* every 14th rnd two more times—184 (192, 204, 216, 224, 244, 264, 284, 304) sts.
Cont to work as est for 14 more rnds, ending after Rnd 18 (18, 18, 18, 16, 16, 16, 12, 10) of Frost Flowers; pc meas approx 9 (9, 9, 11¾, 11¾, 11¼, 11)" from beg.

Next rnd *inc rnd:* K1, m1-L, work to 1 st before side m, m1-R, k1, sl m, k1, m1-L, work to last st, m1-R, k1 (4 sts inc'd)—188 (196, 208, 220, 228, 248, 268, 288, 308) sts.
Rep *inc rnd* every 12th rnd 2 (2, 2, 1, 1, 1, 0, 0, 0) more time(s), then every 10th rnd 0 (0, 0, 1, 1, 1, 1, 1, 0) time(s), then every 8th rnd 0 (0, 0, 0, 0, 1, 1, 2) time(s)—196 (204, 216, 228, 236, 256, 276, 296, 316) sts.

Cont to work as est for 11 (9, 7, 7, 7, 5, 5, 1, 5) more rnd(s), ending after Rnd 6 (4, 2, 24, 22, 20, 16, 8, 8) of Frost Flowers [102 (100, 98, 96, 118, 116, 112, 104, 104) rnds in Frost Flower panel worked to here]; pc meas approx 13¼ (13, 12¾, 12½, 15¼, 15, 14½, 13½, 13½)" from beg.

Begin underarm bind-off

Next rnd: Work as est to last 5 (5, 5, 6, 6, 6, 7, 7, 8) sts, BO 10 (10, 10, 12, 12, 12, 14, 14, 16) sts, removing BOR marker.
Next rnd: Work as est to 5 (5, 5, 6, 6, 6, 7, 7, 8) sts before side marker, BO 10 (10 , 10, 12, 12, 12, 14, 14, 16) sts, removing side marker, knit to end—88 (92, 98, 102, 106, 116, 124, 134, 142) sts rem on each side.

Sleeves

For IMOGEN SPRING, above the elbow sleeves:
With dpns and using the long-tail cast on, CO 57 (58, 60, 62, 65, 67, 69, 73, 75) sts. Pm for BOR and join to work in the rnd, being careful not to twist sts.

Begin garter stitch cuff

First rnd: Purl.
Next rnd: Knit.
Rep last 2 rnds two more times.

Begin stockinette stitch

Next rnd: Knit.
Cont in St st in the rnd until pc meas approx 1" from beg.

Begin sleeve shaping

Next rnd *inc rnd:* K1, m1-L, knit to last st, m1-R, k1 (2 sts inc'd)—59 (60, 62, 64, 67, 69, 71, 75, 77) sts.
Rep *inc rnd* every other rnd 0 (0, 0, 0, 0, 0, 1, 3, 7) time(s), every 4th rnd 0 (0, 0, 0, 0, 6, 10, 9, 7) times, every 6th rnd 3 (7, 7, 7, 7, 3, 0, 0, 0) times, then every 8th rnd 3 (0, 0, 0, 0, 0, 0, 0, 0) times—71 (74, 76, 78, 81, 87, 93, 99, 105) sts.
Cont in St st until sleeve meas approx 8" from beg. Skip to All sleeve lengths on next page.

Beg For IMOGEN WOOL, longer sleeves:

With dpns and using the long-tail cast on, CO 57 (58, 58, 58, 61, 63, 65, 67, 69) sts. Pm for BOR and join to work in the rnd, being careful not to twist sts.

Begin garter stitch cuff

First rnd: Purl.
Next rnd: Knit.
Rep last 2 rnds two more times.

Begin stockinette stitch

Next rnd: Knit.
Cont in St st in the rnd until pc meas approx 4 (4, 4, 4, 4, 4, 3¼, 3¼, 3¼)" from beg.

Begin sleeve shaping

Next rnd *inc rnd:* K1, m1-L, knit to last st, m1-R, k1 (2 sts inc'd)—59 (60, 60, 60, 63, 65, 67, 69, 71) sts.
Rep *inc rnd* every 6th rnd 0 (0, 0, 0, 0, 0, 0, 4, 12) more times, every 8th rnd 0 (0, 0, 0, 0, 6, 11,

11, 5) times, every 12th rnd 0 (1, 5, 9, 9, 5, 2, 0, 0) time(s), every16th rnd 2 (6, 3, 0, 0, 0, 0, 0, 0) times, every 18th rnd 4 (0, 0, 0, 0, 0, 0, 0, 0) times—71 (74, 76, 78, 81, 87, 93, 99, 105) sts. Cont in St st until sleeve meas 18½" from beg.

All sleeve lengths:
Begin underarm bind-off
Next rnd: Knit to last 5 (5, 5, 6, 6, 6, 7, 7, 8) sts, BO 10 (10, 10, 12, 12, 12, 14, 14, 16) sts—61 (64, 66, 66, 69, 75, 79, 85, 89) sts rem.
Next rnd: Knit to end.
Slip sts to waste yarn; break yarn. Set aside.
Repeat for second sleeve.

Yoke
Join sleeve sts to body
Next rnd: With body sts still on circ, pm for BOR, k61 (64, 66, 66, 69, 75, 79, 85, 89) sleeve sts to yoke, pm, work across 88 (92, 98, 102, 106, 116, 124, 134, 142) front sts as est, pm, k61 (64, 66, 66, 69, 75, 79, 85, 89) sleeve sts to yoke, pm, k88 (92, 98, 102, 106, 116, 124, 134, 142) sts across back—298 (312, 328, 336, 350, 382, 406, 438, 462) sts total.
As you proceed with the yoke, continue working Frost Flowers between markers as est, all other sts are worked in St st.
Work for 3 (3, 3, 3, 1, 1, 1, 1, 1) rnd(s) even.

Begin raglan shaping
Next rnd dec rnd: *K1, k2tog, work to 3 sts before next ralgan marker, ssk, k1, sl m; rep from * 3 times (8 sts dec'd)—290 (304, 320, 328, 342, 374, 398, 430, 454) sts rem.
Rep dec rnd every 4th rnd 2 (2, 1, 1, 2, 0, 0, 0, 0) time(s), then every other rnd 19 (20, 23, 24, 24, 28, 29, 33, 30) times, then every rnd 0 (0, 0, 0, 0, 2, 4, 4, 10) times—122 (128, 128, 128, 134, 134, 134, 134, 134) sts rem. [44 (46, 48, 50, 52, 54, 56, 58, 60) sts for front and back, 17 (18, 16, 14, 15, 13, 11, 9, 7) sts for sleeve].

Work even for 1 rnd, ending after Rnd 12 of Frost Flowers [156 (156, 156, 156, 180, 180, 180, 180, 180) rnds of Frost Flowers worked to here].

Begin garter stitch
Next rnd: Purl.
Next rnd: Knit.
Rep last 2 rnds one more time.
Next rnd: Purl.

Next rnd: BO all sts knitwise.

Finishing
Sew underarm seams. Weave in loose ends. Steam or wet block pc to measurements.

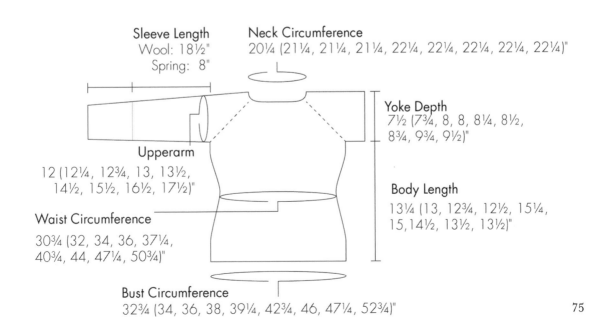

Sleeve Length
Wool: 18½"
Spring: 8"

Neck Circumference
20¼ (21¼, 21¼, 21¼, 22¼, 22¼, 22¼, 22¼, 22¼)"

Yoke Depth
7½ (7¾, 8, 8, 8¼, 8½, 8¾, 9¾, 9½)"

Upperarm
12 (12¼, 12¾, 13, 13½, 14½, 15½, 16½, 17½)"

Body Length
13¼ (13, 12¾, 12½, 15¼, 15,14½, 13½, 13½)"

Waist Circumference
30¾ (32, 34, 36, 37¼, 40¾, 44, 47¼, 50¾)"

Bust Circumference
32¾ (34, 36, 38, 39¼, 42¾, 46, 47¼, 52¾)"

imogen cowl

Finished Measurements
Approx 11½" wide, 51" long

Yarn
Tern by Quince & Co.
(75% American wool, 25% silk); 221yds
[202m]/50g
• 3 skeins in Oyster
OR 555 yds fingering weight yarn

Needles
• One pair straight needles in size US 5 [3.75 mm]
Or size needed to obtain gauge

Notions
• Waste yarn
• Tapestry needle to weave in ends

Gauge
One repeat (34 sts) = 5¼" at widest point, one
repeat (24 rows) = 3", blocked open.

Note
Cowl is worked back and forth in rows, then
seamed together.

Cowl
Using waste yarn, or main yarn and provisional cast
on, CO 74 sts.

Begin Frost Flowers and garter stitch border
(Also, see chart page 77)
Row 1: (RS) K3, *k3, k2tog, k4, yo, p2, [k2, yo,
ssk] 3 times, p2, yo, k4, ssk, k3; rep from *,
end k3.
Row 2: K3, *p2, p2tog-b, p4, yo, p1, k2, [p2,
yo, p2tog] 3 times, k2, p1, yo, p4, p2tog, p2; rep
from *, end k3.
Row 3: K3, *k1, k2tog, k4, yo, k2, p2, [k2, yo,
ssk] 3 times, p2, k2, yo, k4, ssk, k1; rep from *,
end k3.
Row 4: K3, *p2tog-b, p4, yo, p3, k2, [p2, yo,
p2tog] 3 times, k2, p3, yo, p4, p2tog; rep from *,
end k3.
Rows 5–12: Rep Rows 1–4 two times.
Row 13: K3, *yo, ssk, k2, yo, ssk, p2, yo, k4, ssk,
k6, k2tog, k4, yo, p2, k2, yo, ssk, k2; rep from *,
end, k3.
Row 14: K3, *yo, p2tog, p2, yo, p2tog, k2, p1,
yo, p4, p2tog, p4, p2tog-b, p4, yo, p1, k2, p2,
yo, p2tog, p2; rep from *, end k3.

Row 15: K3, *yo, ssk, k2, yo, ssk, p2, k2, yo, k4,
ssk, k2, k2tog, k4, yo, k2, p2, k2, yo, ssk, k2; rep
from *, end k3.
Row 16: K3, *yo, p2tog, p2, yo, p2tog, k2, p3,
yo, p4, p2tog, p2tog-b, p4, yo, p3, k2, p2, yo,
p2tog, p2; rep from *, end k3.
Rows 17–24: Rep Rows 13–16 two times.
Cont to work Rows 1–24 as est until pc meas
approx 51" from beg, ending after Row 24 of
Frost Flowers.

Begin three-needle bind off
Remove waste yarn from CO edge and slip sts onto
open needle. With the right sides of cowl together
(to form ridge on inside of garment), hold the needles
parallel. With a third needle, knit the first st of front
and back needles together, *knit next st from each
needle together (2 sts on RH needle), lift the first st
over the second st and off the RH needle to BO 1 st;
rep from * until all sts are bound off.

Finishing
Weave in ends. Steam or wet block pc
to measurements.

imogen cowl

Key

☐ knit on RS, purl on WS

⊟ purl on RS, knit on WS

⊡ yo

☑ k2tog on RS, p2tog on WS

☒ ssk on RS, p2tog-tbl on WS

◻ pattern repeat

Frost Flowers

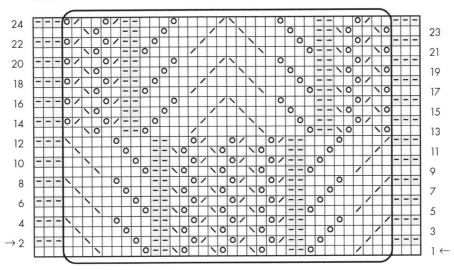

---

immie blanket

Frost Flowers

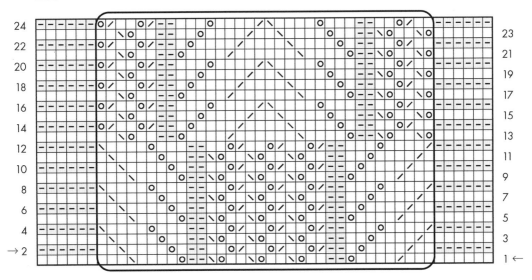

immie blanket

Finished Measurements
23" wide, 23" high

Yarn
Osprey by Quince & Co. (100% American wool)
- 2 skeins in Egret *(blanket 2 entire skeins)*
OR 340 yds aran weight yarn

Needles
- One 32" circular needle (circ) in size US 10½ [6.5 mm]

Or size needed to obtain gauge

Notions
- Tapestry needle for weaving in ends

Gauge
One repeat (34 sts) = 10" at widest point, one repeat high (24 rows) = 5".

Notes
Circular needle is used to accommodate large number of stitches. Blanket is worked back and forth in rows.

Blanket
Using the long-tail cast on, CO 80 sts. Do not join.

Begin garter stitch border
First row: (RS) Knit.
Cont in garter st for 9 more rows, ending after a WS row.

Begin Frost Flowers and continue garter stitch border
(Also, see chart page 77)
Row 1: (RS) K6, *k3, k2tog, k4, yo, p2, [k2, yo, ssk] 3 times, p2, yo, k4, ssk, k3; rep from *, end k6.
Row 2: K6, *p2, p2tog-b, p4, yo, p1, k2, [p2, yo, p2tog] 3 times, k2, p1, yo, p4, p2tog, p2; rep from *, end k6.
Row 3: K6, *k1, k2tog, k4, yo, k2, p2, [k2, yo, ssk] 3 times, p2, k2, yo, k4, ssk, k1; rep from *, end k6.
Row 4: K6, *p2tog-b, p4, yo, p3, k2, [p2, yo, p2tog] 3 times, k2, p3, yo, p4, p2tog; rep from *, end k6.

Rows 5–12: Rep Rows 1–4 two times.
Row 13: K6, *yo, ssk, k2, yo, ssk, p2, yo, k4, ssk, k6, k2tog, k4, yo, p2, k2, yo, ssk, k2; rep from *, end, k6.
Row 14: K6, *yo, p2tog, p2, yo, p2tog, k2, p1, yo, p4, p2tog, p4, p2tog-b, p4, yo, p1, k2, p2, yo, p2tog, p2; rep from *, end k6.
Row 15: K6, *yo, ssk, k2, yo, ssk, p2, k2, yo, k4, ssk, k2, k2tog, k4, yo, k2, p2, k2, yo, ssk, k2; rep from *, end k6.
Row 16: K6, * yo, p2tog, p2, yo, p2tog, k2, p3, yo, p4, p2tog, p2tog-b, p4, yo, p3, k2, p2, yo, p2tog, p2; rep from *, end k6.
Rows 17–24: Rep Rows 13–16 two times.
Rep Rows 1–24 three more times, blanket meas approx 21½" from beg.

Begin garter stitch border
Next row: (RS) Knit.
Cont in garter st for 9 more rows, ending after a WS row.

Next row: (RS) BO all sts knitwise.

Finishing
Weave in ends. Wet block pc to measurements.

immie tee

Finished Chest Measurements
19¾ (21, 22¼, 23½, 24) (24¾, 26½, 27¾, 29½)"
To fit sizes: 6 months (9m, 12m, 18m, 24m) (4 years, 6y, 8y, 10y)
Shown in size 24¾"

Yarn
Tern by Quince & Co. (75% American wool, 25% silk; 221yds [202m] /50g)
• 2 (2, 2, 2, 2) (2, 3, 4, 4) skeins in Mist
OR 265 (285, 310, 395, 425) (435, 535, 665, 700) yds fingering weight yarn

Needles
• One 16" and 24" circular needle (circ) in size US 3 [3.25 mm]
• One set dpns in size US 3 [3.25 mm]
Or size needed to obtain gauge

Notions
• Stitch markers in 3 different colors
• Waste yarn
• Tapestry needle

Gauge
26 sts and 36 rnds = 4" in stockinette stitch, blocked.

Notes
1. Tee is worked from the bottom up with raglan shaping in the yoke.
2. Pattern requires 2 stitch markers to indicate front raglan shaping, 2 markers to indicate sleeve and back raglan shaping, and 2 markers to indicate stitches worked in frost flowers panel.

Frost Flowers (panel of 36 sts)
(Also, see chart page 72)
Rnd 1: K1, yo, ssk, k2, yo, ssk, p2, yo, k4, ssk, k6, k2tog, k4, yo, p2, k2, yo, ssk, k3.
Rnd 2: P1, k2, k2tog, yo, k2, p2, k1, yo, k4, ssk, k4, k2tog, k4, yo, k1, p2, k2tog, yo, k2, k2tog, yo, p1.
Rnd 3: K1, yo, ssk, k2, yo, ssk, p2, k2, yo, k4, ssk, k2, k2tog, k4, yo, k2, p2, k2, yo, ssk, k3.
Rnd 4: P1, k2, k2tog, yo, k2, p2, k3, yo, k4, ssk, k2tog, k4, yo, k3, p2, k2tog, yo, k2, k2tog, yo, p1.
Rnds 5–12: Rep Rows 1—4 two more times.
Rnd 13: K4, k2tog, k4, yo, p2, [k2, yo, ssk] 3 times, p2, yo, k4, ssk, k4.

Rnd 14: P1, k2, k2tog, k4, yo, k1, p2, [k2tog, yo, k2] three times, p2, k1, yo, k4, ssk, k2, p1.
Rnd 15: K2, k2tog, k4, yo, k2, p2, [k2, yo, ssk)] three times, p2, k2, yo, k4, ssk, k2.
Rnd 16: P1, k2tog, k4, yo, k3, p2, [k2tog, yo, k2] three times, p2, k3, yo, k4, ssk, p1.
Rnds 17–24: Rep Rnds 13–16 two more times.
Work Rnds 1–24 for Frost Flowers.

Tee
Body
Using the long-tail cast on, CO 128 (136, 144, 152, 156) (160, 172, 180, 192) sts. Place marker (pm) for BOR and join to work in the rnd, being careful not to twist sts.

Begin garter stitch
Rnd 1: Purl.
Rnd 2: Knit.
Rep Rnds 1 and 2 one more time.

Begin Frost Flowers and stockinette stitch

Next rnd *place markers:* K14 (16, 18, 20, 21) (22, 25, 27, 30), pm for Frost Flowers, work 36 sts in Rnd 1 of Frost Flowers, pm for Frost Flowers, k14 (16, 18, 20, 21) (22, 25, 27, 30) sts, pm for side, k64 (68, 72, 76, 78) (80, 86, 90, 96) sts to end.

Cont to work as est for 47 (45, 43, 63, 61) (61, 81, 101, 97) more rnds, ending after Rnd 24 (22, 20, 16, 14) (14, 10, 6, 2) of Frost Flowers; 48 (46, 44, 64, 62) (62, 82, 102, 98) rnds of Frost Flowers worked to here; pc meas approx 5¼ (5, 5, 7, 7) (7, 9, 11¼, 11)" from beg.

Begin underarm bind-off

Next rnd: Work as est to last 3 (3, 3, 4, 4) (4, 4, 5, 5) sts, BO 6 (6, 6, 8, 8) (8, 8, 10, 10) sts, removing BOR marker.

Next rnd: Work as est to 3 (3, 3, 4, 4) (4, 4, 5, 5) sts before side marker, BO 6 (6, 6, 8, 8) (8, 8, 10, 10) sts, removing side marker, knit to end—58 (62, 66, 68, 70) (72, 78, 80, 86) sts rem on each side. Set aside.

Sleeves

With dpns and using the long-tail cast on, CO 44 (48, 51, 54, 57) (57, 59, 62, 64) sts. Pm for BOR and join to work in the rnd, being careful not to twist sts.

Begin garter stitch cuff

Rnd 1: Purl.
Rnd 2: Knit.
Rep Rnds 1 and 2 one more time.

Next rnd: Knit to last 3 (3, 3, 4, 4, 4) (4, 4, 5, 5) sts, BO 6 (6, 6, 8, 8, 8) (8, 8, 10, 10) sts—38 (42, 45, 46, 49) (49, 51, 52, 54) sts rem.
Next rnd: Knit to end.
Slip sts to waste yarn; break yarn.
Repeat for second sleeve.

Yoke

Join sleeve sts to body

Joining rnd: With longer circ, pm for BOR, k38 (42, 45, 46, 49) (49, 51, 52, 54) sleeve sts, pm, work 58 (62, 66, 68, 70) (72, 78, 80, 86) front sts as est, pm, k38 (42, 45, 46, 49) (49, 51, 52, 54) sleeve sts, pm, k58 (62, 66, 68, 70) (72, 78, 80,

86) back sts—192 (208, 222, 228, 238) (242, 258, 264, 280) sts total.

As you proceed with the yoke, continue working Frost Flowers between markers as est, all other sts are worked in St st.
Work 3 rnds even.

Begin raglan shaping

Note for sizes 19¾ (21, 22¼, 23½, 24) (24¾, - , - , -)":
Front decreases are not worked at the same rate as back and sleeve decreases. This is due to the width of the frost flowers panel and the limited number of decreases possible. Change to shorter circ, then dpns as necessary.

All sizes begin on the same rnd, then follow instructions for *front dec rnd* and *sleeve and back dec rnd* as written below.

Work *front dec rnd* as follows: Work as est to first raglan marker, slip m, k1, k1tog, work as est to 3 sts before next raglan marker, ssk, k1, work as est to end (2 sts dec'd).

Work *sleeve and back dec rnd* as follows: *K1, k2tog, work as est to 3 sts before next raglan marker, ssk, k1, sl m, work across Front sts as est to next raglan marker, sl m, *k1, k2tog, work as est to next raglan m, ssk, k1; rep from * one time (6 sts dec'd).

All sizes:

Next rnd *decrease rnd:* *K1, k2tog, work to 3 sts before next raglan marker, ssk, k1, sl m; rep from * 3 times (8 sts dec'd)—184 (200, 214, 220, 230) (234, 250, 256, 272) sts rem.

For sizes 19¾ (21, 22¼, 23½, 24) (24¾, - , - , -)"

Rep *front dec rnd* every 4th rnd 6 (5, 4, 5, 5) (4, -, -, -) times, then every other round 2 (5, 8, 8, 9, 9) (11, -, -, -) times; rep *sleeve and back dec rnd* every 4th rnd 1 (0, 0, 2, 2) (2, -, -, -) time(s), then every other rnd 12 (15, 16, 14, 15) (15, -, -, -) times—90 (90, 94, 98, 100) (102, -, -, -) sts total; 30 (30, 32, 34, 34) (36, -, -, -) sts for back, 40 (40, 40, 40, 40) (40, -, -, - sts for front, 10 (10, 11, 12, 13) (13, -, -, -) sts for each sleeve.

For sizes - (-, -, -, -) (-, 26½, 27¾, 29½)"

Rep *decrease rnd* every 4th rnd - (-, -, -, -)(-, 3, 5, 5) times, then every other rnd – (-, -, -, -) (-,15, 13, 15) times— - (-, -, -, -) (-, 106, 112, 112) sts total; - (-, -, -, -) (-, 40, 42, 44) sts for front and back, - (-, -, -, -) (-, 13, 14, 12) sts for each sleeve.

All sizes:

Work 1 rnd even, ending on Rnd 12 of Frost Flowers; 84 (84, 84, 108, 108) (108, 132, 154, 154) rnds of Frost Flowers worked to here.

Begin garter stitch neckband

Next rnd: Purl.
Next rnd: Knit.
Next rnd: Purl.
Next rnd: BO all sts knitwise.

Finishing

Weave in ends. Sew underarm seams. Steam or wet block pc to measurements.

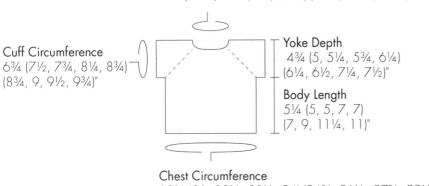

Neck Circumference
13¾ (13¾, 14½, 15, 15½) (15¾, 16¼, 17¼, 17¼)"

Yoke Depth
4¾ (5, 5¼, 5¾, 6¼)
(6¼, 6½, 7¼, 7½)"

Cuff Circumference
6¾ (7½, 7¾, 8¼, 8¾)
(8¾, 9, 9½, 9¾)"

Body Length
5¼ (5, 5, 7, 7)
(7, 9, 11¼, 11)"

Chest Circumference
19¾ (21, 22¼, 23½, 24) (24¾, 26½, 27¾, 29½)"

---

beatrice cardigan

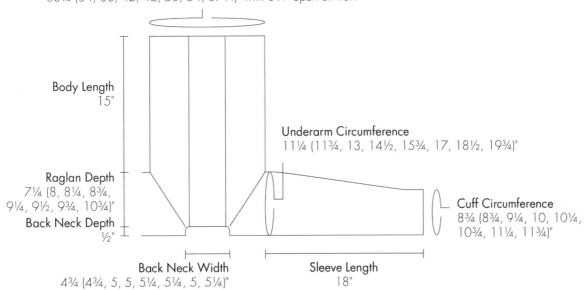

Bust Circumference
30¼ (34, 38, 42, 46, 50, 54, 57¾)" with 3¾" open on front

Body Length
15"

Underarm Circumference
11¼ (11¾, 13, 14½, 15¾, 17, 18½, 19¾)"

Raglan Depth
7¼ (8, 8¼, 8¾, 9¼, 9½, 9¾, 10¾)"

Back Neck Depth
½"

Cuff Circumference
8¾ (8¾, 9¼, 10, 10¼, 10¾, 11¼, 11¾)"

Back Neck Width
4¾ (4¾, 5, 5, 5¼, 5¼, 5, 5¼)"

Sleeve Length
18"

beatrice cardigan

Finished Bust Measurements
30¼ (34, 38, 42, 46, 50, 54, 57¾)" with 3¾"
open at front
Shown in size 34"

Yarn
Lark by Quince & Co.
(100% American wool; 134 yds [123 m]/ 50g)
• 11 (12, 13, 14, 15, 16, 18, 19) skeins in
Chanterelle
OR 1405 (1510, 1660, 1825, 1975, 2130,
2290, 2470) yds worsted weight yarn

Needles
• One 32" circular needle (circ) in size US 7
  [4.5 mm]
• One pair straight needles in size US 7 [4.5 mm]
Or size needed to obtain gauge

Notions
• Stitch markers
• Stitch holders or waste yarn
• Tapestry needle for weaving in ends

Gauge
19 sts and 38 rows = 4" in garter st, blocked.

Cross Stitch (multiple of 8 sts)
Row 1: (RS) *Insert RH needle into next st, wrap
yarn 4 times before pulling the yarn through; rep
from * for each st across.
Row 2: (WS) *With yarn in back, slip 8 sts as if to
purl, dropping all extra wraps; insert LH needle into
the first 4 slipped sts, pass them over the last 4 sts
and onto the LH needle; slip the other 4 sts to the LH
needle; knit the 8 sts in this crossed order; rep from
* across.
Rows 3–6: Knit.
Rep Rows 1–6 for Cross St.

Notes
Cardigan body and sleeves are worked back and
forth in rows from the top down. Circular needle is
used to accommodate large number of stitches.
Band is picked up and worked after body is complete.

Cardigan

Yoke

With circ and using the long-tail cast on, CO 34 (35, 38, 40, 41, 41, 42, 43) sts. Do not join.

Begin garter stitch

First row *place markers*: (WS) K2 (2, 3, 3, 3, 3, 3, 3), pm, k4 (4, 4, 5, 5, 5, 6, 6), pm, k22 (23, 24, 24, 25, 25, 24, 25), pm, k4 (4, 4, 5, 5, 5, 6, 6), pm, k2 (2, 3, 3, 3, 3, 3, 3).

Begin raglan shaping

Set up row *inc row*: (RS) K0 (0, 1, 1, 1, 1, 1, 1), k1-f/b, k1, sl m, k1, k1-f/b, *knit to 2 sts before next m, k1-f/b, k1, sl m, k1, k1-f/b; rep from * 2 more times, k0 (0, 1, 1, 1, 1, 1, 1) [8 sts inc'd]—42 (43, 46, 48, 49, 49, 50, 51) total sts; 3 (3, 4, 4, 4, 4, 4, 4) sts each front, 6 (6, 6, 7, 7, 7, 8, 8) sts each sleeve and 24 (25, 26, 26, 27, 27, 26, 27) sts for back.

Next row: (WS) Knit.

Next row *body and sleeve inc row*: (RS) *Knit to 2 sts before m, k1-f/b, k1, sl m, k1, k1-f/b; rep from * 3 more times, knit to end (8 sts inc'd).
Rep the last 2 rows 9 (6, 10, 12, 16, 20, 22, 24) more times—122 (99, 134, 152, 185, 217, 234, 251) total sts; 13 (10, 15, 17, 21, 25, 27, 29) sts each front, 26 (20, 28, 33, 41, 49, 54, 58) sts each sleeve and 44 (39, 48, 52, 61, 69, 72, 77) sts for back.

Sizes - (34, 38, 42, 46, 50, 54, 57¾)" only:

Next row: (WS) Knit.

Next row *body inc row*: (RS) *Knit to 2 sts before m, k1-f/b, k1, sl m, knit sleeve sts to next m, sl m, k1, k1-f/b; rep from * one more time, knit to end (4 sts inc'd).

Next row: Knit.

Next row *body and sleeve inc row:* (RS) *Knit to 2 sts before m, k1-f/b, k1, sl m, k1, k1-f/b; rep from * 3 more times, knit to end (8 sts inc'd).
Rep the last 4 rows - (2, 3, 5, 6, 8, 10, 11) more times— - (135, (182, 224, 269, 325, 366, 395) total sts; - (16, 23, 29, 35, 43, 49, 53) sts each front, - (26, 36, 45, 55, 67, 76, 82) sts each sleeve and - (51, 64, 76, 89, 105, 116, 125) sts for back.

Sizes 30¼ (34, 38, 42, 46, 50, -, -)" only:

Next 3 rows: Knit.

Next row *body and sleeve inc row:* (RS) *Knit to 2 sts before m, k1-f/b, k1, sl m, k1, k1-f/b; rep from * 3 more times, knit to end (8 sts inc'd).
Rep the last 4 rows 10 (10, 8, 6, 4, 1, -, -) more time(s)—210 (223, 254, 280, 309, 341, -, -) total sts; 24 (27, 32, 36, 40, 45, -, -) sts each front, 48 (48, 54, 59, 65, 71, -, -) sts each sleeve and 66 (73, 82, 90, 99, 109, -, -) sts for back.

All Sizes:

Work 3 (3, 3, 3, 3, 3, 1, 1) row(s) even in garter st, ending after a WS row; yoke meas approx 7¼ (8, 8¼, 8¾, 9¼, 9½, 9¾, 10¾)" from beg.

Begin underarm cast-on

Next row: (RS) K24 (27, 32, 36, 40, 45, 49, 53) front sts to m, remove m, transfer next 48 (48, 54, 59, 65, 71, 76, 82) sleeve sts to st holder or waste yarn, remove m, using backward loop cast on, CO 6 (8, 8, 10, 10, 10, 12, 12) underarm sts, k66 (73, 82, 90, 99, 109, 116, 125) back sts to m, remove m, transfer next 48 (48, 54, 59, 65, 71, 76, 82) sleeve sts to st holder or waste yarn, remove m, using the backward loop cast on, CO 6 (8, 8, 10, 10, 10, 12, 12) underarm sts, k24 (27, 32, 36, 40, 45, 49, 53) front sts to end—126 (143, 162, 182, 199, 219, 238, 255) body sts.

Body

Cont in garter st until body meas approx 7½" from underarm CO, ending after a WS row.

Make pocket openings

Next row: (RS) K1 (3, 5, 7, 9, 11, 13, 15), transfer next 24 sts to st holder or waste yarn for pocket lining, pm, using backward loop cast on, CO 24 sts, pm, knit to last 25 (27, 29, 31, 33, 35, 37, 39) sts, transfer next 24 sts to st holder or waste yarn for pocket lining, pm, using backward loop cast on, CO 24 sts, pm, knit to end.
Work 3 rows even in garter st.

Next row: (RS) *Knit to m, sl m, work next 24 pocket sts in Row 1 of Cross St, sl m; rep from * one time, knit to end.
Next row: (WS) *Knit to m, sl m, work next 24 pocket sts in Row 2 of Cross St, sl m; rep from * one time, knit to end.

Removing pocket markers, cont to work all body sts in garter st until body meas approx 15" from underarm cast on, ending after a WS row.

Next row: (RS) Loosely BO all sts purlwise.

Sleeve

Transfer 48 (48, 54, 59, 65, 71, 76, 82) held sts from one sleeve to circ, do not join; work back and forth in rows. Note: Change to straight needles when comfortable, if desired.

Begin underarm cast-on

Next row: (WS) Using the backwards loop cast on, CO 3 (4, 4, 5, 5, 5, 6, 6) sts, knit to end of held sts, CO another 3 (4, 4, 5, 5, 5, 6, 6) sts—54 (56, 62, 69, 75, 81, 88, 94) sts.

Cont in garter st until sleeve meas approx 1" from underarm, ending after a WS row.

Begin sleeve shaping

Next row *dec row:* (RS) K2, ssk, knit to last 4 sts, k2tog, k2 (2 sts dec'd)—52 (54, 60, 67, 73, 79, 86, 92) sts.
Work even in garter st for 25 (21, 15, 13, 11, 9, 7, 7) rows, ending after a WS row.
Rep the last 26 (22, 16, 14, 12, 10, 8, 8) rows 2 (3, 5, 1, 1, 5, 13, 7) more time(s), then work *dec row* one more time—46 (46, 48, 63, 69, 67, 58, 76) sts.

Work even in garter st for 23 (19, 13, 11, 9, 7, 5, 5) rows, ending after a WS row.

Next row *dec row:* (RS) K2, ssk, knit to last 4 sts, k2tog, k2 (2 sts dec'd)—44 (44, 46, 61, 67, 65, 56, 74) sts.
Rep the last 24 (20, 14, 12, 10, 8, 6, 6) rows 1 (1, 1, 7, 9, 7, 1, 9) more time(s)—42 (42, 44, 47, 49, 51, 54, 56) sts rem.

Cont even in garter st until sleeve meas approx 15" from underarm, ending after a WS row.

Begin Cross Stitch cuff

Next row: (RS) K9 (9, 10, 11, 12, 13, 15, 16), pm, work next 24 sts in Row 1 of Cross St, pm, k9 (9, 10, 12, 13, 14, 15, 16).
Cont as est, working Rows 2–6 of Cross St between markers, and all other sts in garter st.

Work 2 more repeats of Cross St as est. Work Rows 1–5 of Cross St one more time; sleeve meas approx 18" from underarm.

Next row: (WS) Loosely BO all sts knitwise.

Work second sleeve the same as the first.

Pocket lining

Transfer 24 held sts from one pocket to larger needle and join yarn ready to work a RS row.
Next row *inc row:* (RS) K1-f/b, knit to last st, k1-f/b (2 sts inc'd)—26 sts.
Cont in garter st until lining meas approx 5" from pick-up row, ending after a WS row.
Next row: (RS) BO all sts knitwise.

Work second pocket lining the same as the first.

Finishing

Weave in ends. Wet or stream block pc to measurements. Whip stitch pocket linings to body. Seam sleeves and underarms.

Front band

With circ, RS facing, and beg at the lower edge of right front, pick up and knit 106 (110, 109, 112, 111, 115, 119, 122) sts along right front, 32 (32, 34, 36, 38, 38, 38, 40) sts along CO edge of neck, 106 (110, 109, 112, 111, 115, 119, 122) sts along left front—244 (252, 252, 260, 260, 268, 276, 284) sts.

First row: (WS) Knit.
Cont in garter st for 4 more rows (3 garter ridges).

Begin Cross Stitch

Next row: (RS) K2 (edge sts, keep in garter st throughout), work to last 2 sts in Row 1 of Cross St, k2 (edge sts, keep in garter st throughout).

Cont as est, maintaining garter st edge sts and working Rows 2–6 of Cross St over all other sts. Work Rows 1–6 one more time, then Rows 1–5 of Cross St one time, (band meas approx 3¼" from the pick up edge.)
Next row: (WS) Loosely BO all sts knitwise.

Weave in ends. Block again if desired.

beatrice cowl

Finished Measurements
8" wide by 56" long

Yarn
Lark by Quince & Co. (100% American wool, 134 yds [123 m]/50 g)
• 4 skeins in Bird's Egg
OR 430 yds of worsted weight yarn

Needles
• One pair straight needles in size US 7 [4.5 mm]

Or size needed to obtain gauge

Notions
• Waste yarn
• Tapestry needle for weaving in ends

Gauge
18 sts and 28 rows = 4" in garter st, blocked.

Notes
Cowl is worked flat. Ends are joined to make loop. Slip first st of every row in this manner: Slip 1 knitwise with yarn in back.

Cowl
Using waste yarn, or main yarn and the provisional cast on, CO 40 sts.
First row: Knit.

Begin Cross Stitch
Rows 1–8: Sl 1 (see Notes), knit to end.
Row 9: (RS) Sl 1, k3, *insert RH needle into next st, wrap yarn 4 times before pulling the yarn through; rep from * for each st to last 4 sts, k4.
Row 10: (WS) Sl 1, k3, *with yarn in back, slip 8 sts as if to purl, dropping all extra wraps; insert LH needle into the first 4 slipped sts, pass them over the last 4 sts and onto the LH needle; slip the other 4 sts to the LH needle; knit the 8 sts in this crossed order; rep from * to last 4 sts, end k4.
Cont to work Rows 1–10 of Cross St as est until pc measures approximately 56" from beg, ending after Row 10 of Cross St.

Begin three-needle bind off
Remove waste yarn from CO and slip sts onto open needle. With RS of cowl together (to form ridge on inside of garment), hold the needles parallel. With a third needle, knit the first st of front and back needles together, *knit next st from each needle together (2 sts on RH needle), lift the first st over the second st and off the RH needle to BO 1 st; rep from * until all sts are bound off.

Finishing
Weave in ends. Steam block pc to measurements.

bea cardi

Finished Bust Measurements
30 (34, 38, 42, 46, 50, 54, 58)" with 4" overlap
Shown in size 34"

Yarn
Tern by Quince & Co. (75% American wool, 25% silk; 221yds [202m]/50g)
- 6 (7, 8, 8, 9, 10, 11, 11) skeins in Mist
OR 1315 (1460, 1615, 1760, 1920, 2080, 2235, 2400) yds fingering weight yarn

Needles
- One 32" circular needle (circ) in size US 5 [3.75 mm]
- One pair in size US 5 [3.75 mm]

Or size needed to obtain gauge

Notions
- Stitch markers
- Stitch holder or waste yarn
- Tapestry needle for weaving in ends

Gauge
24 sts and 48 rows = 4" in garter st;
28 sts and 32 rows = 4" in Cross St.

Cross Stitch (multiple of 8 sts)
Row 1: (RS) *Insert RH needle into next st, wrap yarn 3 times before pulling the yarn through; rep from * for each st across.
Row 2: (WS) *With yarn in back, slip 8 sts as if to purl, dropping all extra wraps; insert LH needle into the first 4 slipped sts, pass them over the last 4 sts and onto the LH needle; slip the other 4 sts to the LH needle; knit the 8 sts in this crossed order; rep from * across.
Rows 3–8: Knit.
Rep Rows 1–8 for Cross St.

Notes
1. Cardigan body and sleeves are worked back and forth in rows from the top down.
2. Circular needle is used to accommodate large number of stitches. You may want to use different color markers to tell the difference between the cross stitch markers and the raglan markers.
3. Slip first st of every row on yoke and body in this manner: Slip 1 purlwise with yarn in front, bring yarn back ready to knit next stitch.

Cardi
Yoke
With circ and using the long-tail cast on, CO 128 (120, 120, 120, 120, 120, 120, 120) sts. Do not join.

Begin neck band
First row: Sl 1 (see notes), knit to end.
Rep last row 2 more times.

Next row: (RS) Sl 1, k3, work Row 1 of Cross St to last 4 sts, k4.
Next row: (WS) Sl 1, k3, work Row 2 of Cross St to last 4 sts, k4.
Next row *place markers:* (RS) Sl 1, k3, pm for Cross St, work next 32 sts in Row 3 of Cross St, pm for Cross St, k2, pm for raglan, k10 (6, 6, 6, 6, 6, 6, 6) for sleeve, pm for raglan, k32 for back, pm for raglan, k10 (6, 6, 6, 6, 6, 6, 6) for sleeve, pm for raglan, k2, pm for Cross St, work next 32 sts in Row 3 of Cross St, pm for Cross St, k4 to end.

Next row: (WS) Sl 1, k3, sl m, work Row 4 of Cross St between Cross St markers, sl m, knit (slipping raglan markers as you come to them) to next Cross St marker, sl m, work Row 4 of Cross St between Cross St markers, sl m, knit to end.

Begin raglan shaping

As you proceed with the yoke, continue working sts in Cross St and garter st as est, slipping the first st of every row, while working raglan shaping as follows:

Set-up row *inc row:* (RS) *Work as est to 2 sts before raglan m, k1-f/b, k1, sl m, k1, k1-f/b; rep from * 3 more times, work as est to end (8 sts inc'd)—136 (128, 128, 128, 128, 128, 128, 128) sts.

Sizes - (-, -, 42, 46, 50, 54, 58)" only:

Next row *body inc row:* (WS) *Work as est to 2 sts before raglan m, k1-f/b, k1, sl m, work across sleeve sts as est, sl m, k1, k1-f/b, rep from * one time, work as est to end (4 sts inc'd)—- (-, -, 132, 132, 132, 132, 132) sts.

Next row *body and sleeve inc row:* (RS) *Work as est to 2 sts before raglan m, k1-f/b, k1, sl m, k1, k1-f/b; rep from * 3 more times, work as est to end (8 sts inc'd)— - - (-, -, 140, 140, 140, 140, 140) sts.
Rep the last 2 rows - (-, -, 0, 1, 2, 4, 5) more time(s)— - (-, -, 140, 152, 164, 188, 200) total sts; - (-, -, 41, 43, 45, 49, 51) sts each front, - (-, -, 10, 12, 14, 18, 20) sts each sleeve and - (-, -, 38, 42, 46, 54, 58) sts for back.

All Sizes:

Next row: (WS) Work 1 row even as est.
Next row *body and sleeve inc row:* (RS) *Work as est to 2 sts before raglan m, k1-f/b, k1, sl m, k1, k1-f/b; rep from * 3 more times, work as est to end (8 sts inc'd)—144 (136, 136, 148, 160, 172, 196, 208) sts.
Rep the last 2 rows 15 (19, 22, 25, 25, 24, 24, 23) more times—264 (288, 312, 348, 360, 364, 388, 392) total sts; 55 (59, 62, 67, 69, 70, 74, 75) sts each front, 44 (48, 54, 62, 64, 64, 68, 68) sts each sleeve and 66 (74, 80, 90, 94, 96, 104, 106) sts for back.

Sizes - (34, 38, 42, 46, 50, 54, 58)" only:

Next row: (WS) Work 1 row even as est.
Next row *body inc row:* (RS) *Work as est to 2 sts before raglan m, k1-f/b, k1, sl m, work across sleeve sts as est, sl m, k1, k1-f/b, rep from * one

time, work as est to end (4 sts inc'd)—292 (316, 352, 364, 368, 392, 396) sts.
Next row: (WS) Work 1 row even as est.
Next row *body and sleeve inc row:* (RS) *Work as est to 2 sts before raglan m, k1-f/b, k1, sl m, k1, k1-f/b; rep from * 3 more times, work as est to end (8 sts inc'd)—300 (324, 360, 372, 376, 400, 404) sts.
Rep the last 4 rows - (1, 4, 5, 7, 9, 10, 12) more time(s)— - (312, 372, 420, 456, 484, 520, 548) total sts; - (63, 72, 79, 85, 90, 96, 101) sts each front, - (52, 64, 74, 80, 84, 90, 94) sts each sleeve and - (82, 100, 114, 126, 136, 148, 158) sts for back.

Sizes 30 (34, 38, -, -, -, -, -)" only:

Next 3 rows: Work even as est.
Next row: *body and sleeve inc row:* (RS) *Work as est to 2 sts before raglan m, k1-f/b, k1, sl m, k1, k1-f/b; rep from * 3 more times, work as est to end (8 sts inc'd)—272 (320, 380, -, -, -, -, -)sts.
Rep the last 4 rows 6 (4, 1, -, -, -, -, -) more time(s)—320 (352, 388, -, -, -, -, -) total sts; 62 (68, 74, -, -, -, -, -) sts each front, 58 (62, 68, -, -, -, -, -) sts each sleeve and 80 (92, 104, -, -, -, -, -) sts for back.

All Sizes:

320 (352, 388, 420, 456, 484, 520, 548) sts on needle. Work 3 (3, 3, 3, 1, 1, 1, 1) row(s) even as est, ending after a WS row; yoke meas approx 6¼ (6¾, 7¼, 7½, 8½, 9½, 10½, 11½)" from beg.

Begin underarm cast-on

Next row: (RS) Work as est to raglan m, remove m, transfer next 58 (62, 68, 74, 80, 84, 90, 94) sleeve sts to st holder or waste yarn, remove m, using backward loop cast on, CO 10 (10, 10, 12, 12, 14, 14, 16) underarm sts, knit back sts to m, remove m, transfer next 58 (62, 68, 74, 80, 84, 90, 94) sleeve sts to st holder or waste yarn, remove m, using the backward loop cast on, CO 10 (10, 10, 12, 12, 14, 14, 16) underarm sts, work as est to end—224 (248, 272, 296, 320, 344, 368, 392) body sts.

Body

Cont working sts in Cross St and garter st as est, slipping the first st of every row until body meas approx 10¾" from underarm cast on, ending after Row 8 of Cross St.

Begin Cross Stitch across bottom edge

Next row: (RS) Sl 1, k3, work Row 1 of Cross St to last 4 sts (removing markers), k4 to end.
Next row: (WS) Sl 1, k3, work Row 2 of Cross St to last 4 sts, k4 to end.
Next 2 rows: Sl 1, knit to end.
Next row: (RS) Loosely BO all sts knitwise.

Sleeves

Transfer 58 (62, 68, 74, 80, 84, 90, 94) held sts from one sleeve to circ. Do not join; work back and forth in rows. Note: Change to straight needles when comfortable, if desired.

Begin underarm shaping

Next row: (WS) Using the backward loop cast on, CO 5 (5, 5, 6, 6, 7, 7, 8) sts, knit to end of held sts, CO 5 (5, 5, 6, 6, 7, 7, 8) more sts—68 (72, 78, 86, 92, 98, 104, 110) sts.
Cont in garter st until sleeve meas approx 1″ from underarm CO, ending after a WS row.

Begin sleeve shaping

Next row *dec row*: (RS) K2, ssk, knit to last 4 sts, k2tog, k2 (2 sts dec'd)—66 (70, 76, 84, 90, 96, 102, 108) sts.

Work even in garter st for 25 (21, 15, 11, 9, 7, 5, 5) rows, ending after a WS row.
Rep the last 26 (22, 16, 12, 10, 8, 6, 6) rows 2 (3, 5, 7, 9, 11, 13, 15) more times, then work *dec row* one more time—60 (62, 64, 68, 70 72, 74, 76) sts rem.

Cont even in garter st until sleeve meas approx 10″ from underarm, ending after a WS row.

Begin Cross Stitch edge

Next row: (RS) K2 (3, 4, 2, 3, 4, 1, 2), work Row 1 of Cross St to last 2 (3, 4, 2, 3, 4, 1, 2) sts, knit to end.
Next row: (WS) K2 (3, 4, 2, 3, 4, 1, 2), work Row 2 of Cross St to last 2 (3, 4, 2, 3, 4, 1, 2) sts, knit to end.
Next 2 rows: Knit.
Next row: (RS) Loosely BO all sts knitwise.

Work second sleeve the same as the first.

Finishing

Weave in ends. Steam block pc to measurements. Seam sleeves and underarms.

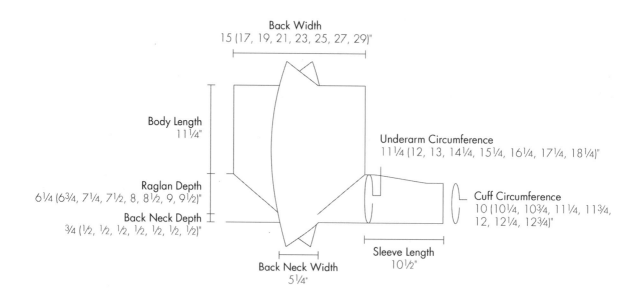

Back Width
15 (17, 19, 21, 23, 25, 27, 29)″

Body Length
11¼″

Underarm Circumference
11¼ (12, 13, 14¼, 15¼, 16¼, 17¼, 18¼)″

Cuff Circumference
10 (10¼, 10¾, 11¼, 11¾, 12, 12¼, 12¾)″

Raglan Depth
6¼ (6¾, 7¼, 7½, 8, 8½, 9, 9½)″

Back Neck Depth
¾ (½, ½, ½, ½, ½, ½, ½)″

Sleeve Length
10½″

Back Neck Width
5¼″

beatrice wrap

Finished Measurements
54" wide x 28" high

Yarn
Lark by Quince & Co. (100% American wool; 134 yds [123 m]/50 g)
• 11 skeins in Sedum
OR 1400 yds of worsted weight yarn

Needles
• One 40" circular needle (circ) in size US 7 [4.5 mm]
Or size needed to obtain gauge

Notions
• Tapestry needle for weaving in ends

Gauge
18 sts and 28 rows = 4" in garter st, blocked.

Notes
Circular needle is used to accommodate large number of stitches. Slip first st of every row in this manner: Slip 1 knitwise with yarn in back.

Wrap
Using the long-tail cast on, CO 256 sts. Do not join.

Begin garter stitch
First row: (RS) Sl1 (see Notes), knit to end.
Rep last row 6 more times.

Begin Cross Stitch
Rows 1–6: Sl 1, knit to end.
Row 7: (RS) Sl 1, k7, *insert RH needle into next st, wrap yarn 4 times before pulling the yarn through;

rep from * for each st to last 8 sts, k8.
Row 8: (WS) Sl 1, k7, *with yarn in back, slip 8 sts as if to purl, dropping all extra wraps; insert LH needle into the first 4 slipped sts, pass them over the last 4 sts and onto the LH needle; slip the other 4 sts to the LH needle; knit the 8 sts in this crossed order; rep from * to last 8 sts, end k8.
Cont to work Rows 1–8 of as est 18 more times, then work Rows 1–6 one time.

Begin garter stitch
Next row: (RS) Sl 1, knit to end.
Rep last row 7 more times.

Next row: (WS) BO all sts knitwise.

Finishing
Weave in ends. Block to measurements.

---

beatrice scarf

Finished Measurements
9½" wide by 82" long

Yarn
Canopy Worsted by The Fibre Co. (50% baby alpaca, 30% merino wool + 20% viscose from bamboo; 200 yds [183 m]/100 g)
• 3 skeins in Quetzal
OR
575 yds worsted weight yarn

Needles
• One pair straight needles in size US 7 [4.5 mm]
Or size needed to obtain gauge
Notions
• Tapestry needle for weaving in ends
Gauge
19 sts and 28 rows = 4" in garter st, blocked.

Note
Slip first st of every row in this manner: Slip 1 knitwise with yarn in back.

Scarf
Using the long-tail cast on, CO 48 sts.

Begin garter stitch
First row: (RS) Sl1 (see Note), knit to end.
Rep last row one time.

Begin Cross Stitch
Rows 1–6: Sl 1, knit to end.
Row 7: (RS) Sl 1, k3, *insert RH needle into next st, wrap yarn 4 times before pulling the yarn through; rep from * for each st to last 4 sts, k4.

Row 8: (WS) Sl 1, k3, *with yarn in back, slip 8 sts as if to purl, dropping all extra wraps; insert LH needle into the first 4 slipped sts, pass them over the last 4 sts and onto the LH needle; slip the other 4 sts to the LH needle; knit the 8 sts in this crossed order; rep from * to last 4 sts, end k4.
Rep Rows 1–8 for Cross St.
Work all sts in Rows 1–8 of Cross St until scarf meas approx 75" from beg, ending after Row 8 of Cross St. (Scarf will grow in length once wet-blocked.)

Begin garter stitch
Next row: (RS) Sl 1, knit to end.
Rep last row 6 more times.

Next row: (WS) BO all sts knitwise.

Finishing
Weave in ends. Wet block pc to measurements.

---

bea tee

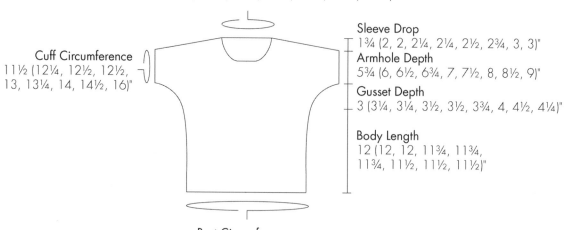

Neck Circumference
19¾ (19¾, 21¼, 21¼, 22¾, 24½, 24½, 24½, 24½)"

Sleeve Drop
1¾ (2, 2, 2¼, 2¼, 2½, 2¾, 3, 3)"
Armhole Depth
5¾ (6, 6½, 6¾, 7, 7½, 8, 8½, 9)"

Cuff Circumference
11½ (12¼, 12½, 12½, 13, 13¼, 14, 14½, 16)"

Gusset Depth
3 (3¼, 3¼, 3½, 3½, 3¾, 4, 4½, 4¼)"

Body Length
12 (12, 12, 11¾, 11¾, 11¾, 11½, 11½, 11½)"

Bust Circumference
35¾ (38¾, 42, 45, 48, 51, 54¾, 57¼, 60¼)"

bea tee

Finished Bust Measurements
35¾ (38¾, 42, 45, 48, 51, 54¾, 57¼, 60¼)"
Shown in size 38¾"

Yarn
Firefly by Classic Elite Yarns (25% linen, 75% viscose; 155 yds [142 m]/50g)
• 6 (6, 7, 7, 8, 8, 9, 10, 11) skeins in Britannia OR 810 (905, 990, 1075, 1160, 1250, 1370, 1500, 1565) yds sport weight yarn

Needles
• One 24" circular needle (circ) in size US 4 [3.5 mm]
• One 16" circ in size US 3 [3.25 mm]
• One set of dpns in size US 3 [3.25 mm]
Or size needed to obtain gauge

Notions
• Stitch markers
• Contrasting yarn for Sunday Short Rows
• Stitch holders or waste yarn
• Tapestry needle for weaving in ends

Gauge
21 sts and 31 rows = 4" in St st with larger needle, blocked.

Cross Stitch (multiple of 8)
Row 1: (WS) Knit.
Rows 2 and 3: Knit.
Row 4: (RS) *Insert RH needle into next st, wrap yarn 3 times before pulling the yarn through; rep from * for each st across.
Row 5: (WS) *With yarn in back, slip 8 sts as if to purl, dropping all extra wraps; insert LH needle into the first 4 slipped sts, pass them over the last 4 sts and onto the LH needle; slip the other 4 sts to the LH needle; knit the 8 sts in this crossed order; rep from * across.
Row 6–8: Knit.

Notes
Tee is worked in one piece from the bottom up to the underarm, then front and back are worked separately to the shoulder. Shoulders are shaped using Sunday Short Rows (For more info on this see Techniques pg 94 for link to Carol Sunday's website) and joined using the three-needle bindoff.

Tee
Back
With longer circ and using the long-tail cast on, CO 188 (204, 220, 236, 252, 268, 288, 300, 316) sts. Place marker (pm) for BOR and join to work in the rnd, being careful not to twist sts.

Begin garter stitch
First rnd: Purl.
Next rnd: Knit.
Next rnd: Purl.

Begin stockinette stitch
Next rnd: Knit.
Cont in St st in the rnd until pc meas 12 (12, 12, 11¾, 11¾, 11¾, 11½, 11½, 11½)" from beg.

Next rnd *place marker:* K94 (102, 110, 118, 126, 134, 144, 150, 158) sts, pm for side, k 94 (102, 110, 118, 126, 134, 144, 150, 158) sts to end.

Begin sleeve shaping

Note: Front and back will be worked separately, back and forth in rows from here to shoulder.

Next row *inc row:* (RS) K1, m1, knit to 1 st before side m, m1, k1, turn (2 sts inc'd)— 96 (104, 112, 120, 128, 136, 146, 152, 160) sts for front. Place 94 (102, 110, 118, 126, 134, 144, 150, 158) back sts onto waste yarn.

Next row: (WS) Purl.

Work in St st for 2 more rows.

Rep *inc row* this next row, then every 4th row 3 times, then every other row 3 times— 108 (116, 124, 132, 140, 148, 158, 164, 172 sts.

Next row: (WS) Using the backward loop cast on, CO 2 sts at end of next 2 (4, 4, 6, 6, 8, 10, 14, 12) rows—112 (124, 132, 144, 152, 164, 178, 192, 196) sts.

Final sleeve cast on: (WS) CO 16 sts at end of next 2 rows—144 (156, 164, 176, 184, 196, 210, 224, 228 sts.

Next row: (WS) Purl.

Next row: (RS) Knit.

Cont in St st until pc meas 3½ (3¾, 4¼, 4½, 4½, 4½, 5¾, 6, 6¾)" from final sleeve CO, ending after a WS row.

Begin neck shaping

Next row: (RS) Place removable markers outside center 22 (22, 22, 22, 24, 24, 26, 26, 26) sts, then knit to first m, BO 22 (22, 22, 22, 24, 24, 26, 26, 26) sts, removing markers, knit to end—61 (67, 71, 77, 80, 86, 92, 99, 101) sts each side.

Next row: (WS) Working both sides at the same time, purl to neck edge, attach new ball of yarn on other side, BO 2 (2, 3, 3, 3, 3, 3, 3, 3) sts, purl to end.

Next row: (RS) Knit to neck edge, BO 2 (2, 3, 3, 3, 3, 3, 3, 3) sts, on other side knit to end—59 (65, 68, 74, 77, 83, 90, 96, 98) sts each side.

BO 0 (0, 2, 2, 2, 2, 2, 2, 2) sts at the beg of the next 0 (0, 2, 2, 2, 2, 2, 2, 2) rows—59 (65, 66, 72, 75, 81, 87, 94, 96) sts each side.

Next row: (WS) Purl.

Next row *dec row:* (RS) Knit to 4 sts before neck edge, k2tog, k2; on other side, k2, ssk, knit to end (1 st dec'd at each neck edge)—58 (64, 65, 71, 74, 80, 86, 93, 95) sts each side.

Rep *dec row* every other row 2 (2, 2, 2, 3, 3, 3, 3, 3) more times, then every 4th row 2 (3, 2, 3, 3, 4, 3, 3, 3) times— 54 (59, 61, 66, 68, 73, 80, 87, 89) sts rem each side; **and at the same time, when pc meas 5¾ (6, 6¼, 6¼, 6½, 6¾, 7, 7¼, 8)" from final sleeve cast on, begin shoulder short-row shaping:**

Note: Continue to work both left front and right front at the same time.

Short Row 1: (RS) Knit to last 6 (5, 6, 5, 6, 5, 5, 5, 6) sts, turn work, place one strip of CC yarn across working yarn as for a Sunday Short Row.

Short Row 2: (WS) Purl to last 6 (5, 6, 5, 6, 5, 5, 5, 6) sts, turn work, place one strip of CC yarn across working yarn as for a Sunday Short Row.

Short Row 3: Knit to 6 (7, 7, 8, 8, 9, 10, 11, 11) sts before previous turning point, turn work, place one strip of CC yarn across working yarn.

Short Row 4: Purl to 6 (7, 7, 8, 8, 9, 10, 11, 11) sts before previous turning point, turn work, place one strip of CC yarn across working yarn.

Rep last 2 short rows 5 (6, 6, 7, 7, 8, 9, 10, 10) more times.

After final turning point, knit to end of row and resolve short rows as for a RS row.

Purl 1 row and resolve short rows as for a WS row.

Slip sts to waste yarn or holder.

Back
Begin sleeve shaping

Transfer 94 (102, 110, 118, 126, 134, 144, 150, 158) back sts onto circ and attach new ball of yarn, ready to work a RS row.

Next row *inc row:* (RS) K1, m1, knit to last st, m1, k1, turn (2 sts inc'd)—96 (104, 112, 120, 128, 136, 146, 152, 160) sts for back.

Next row: (WS) Purl.

Work in St st for 2 more rows.

Rep *inc row* this next row, then every 4th row 3 times, then every other row 3 times— 108 (116, 124, 132, 140, 148, 158, 164, 172) sts.

Next row: (WS) Using the backward loop cast on, CO 2 sts at end of next 2 (4, 4, 6, 6, 8, 10, 14, 12) rows—112 (124, 132, 144, 152, 164, 178, 192, 196) sts.

Final sleeve cast on: (WS) CO 16 sts at end of next 2 rows—144 (156, 164, 176, 184, 196, 210, 224, 228 sts.

Next row: (WS) Purl.
Next row: (RS) Knit.
Cont in St st until pc meas 5¾ (6, 6¼, 6¼, 6½, 6¾, 7, 7¼, 8)" from final sleeve CO, ending after a WS row.

Short Row 1: (RS) Knit to last 6 (5, 6, 5, 6, 5, 5, 5, 6) sts, turn work, place one strip of CC yarn across working yarn as for a Sunday Short Row.
Short Row 2: (WS) Purl to last 6 (5, 6, 5, 6, 5, 5, 5, 6) sts, turn work, place one strip of CC yarn across working yarn as for a Sunday Short Row.
Short Row 3: Knit to 6 (7, 7, 8, 8, 9, 10, 11, 11 sts before previous turning point, turn work, place one strip of CC yarn across working yarn.
Short Row 4: Purl to 6 (7, 7, 8, 8, 9, 10, 11, 11) sts before previous turning point, turn work, place one strip of CC yarn across working yarn.
Rep last 2 short rows 5 (6, 6, 7, 7, 8, 9, 10, 10) more times.
After final turning point, knit to end of row and resolve short rows as for a RS row.

Next row: Purl to neck edge, BO center 36 (38, 42, 44, 48, 50, 50, 50, 50) sts, purl to last st, resolving short rows as you come to them as for a WS.
Slip sts onto stitch holder or waste yarn. Do not break yarn.

Finishing
Block pc to measurements.

Begin three-needle bind off
Transfer front sts to an open needle. With the RS of

each shoulder together (to form ridge on inside of garment), hold the needles parallel. With a third needle, knit the first st of front and back needles together, *knit next st from each needle together (2 sts on RH needle), lift the first st over the second st and off the RH needle to BO 1 st; rep from * until all sts are bound off.

Sew sleeve seams from cuff to underarm.

Begin neckband
With shorter circ, at center back neck, RS facing, pick up and knit 18 (19, 21, 22, 24, 25, 25, 25, 25) sts along neck edge for half the back and 70 (68, 72, 70, 74, 80, 80, 80, 80) sts along the front neck edge, then 18 (19, 21, 22, 24, 25, 25, 25, 25) sts along other half of back neck—106 (106, 114, 114, 122, 130, 130, 130, 130) sts. Do not join.

Begin Cross Stitch
First row: (WS) K1 (seam st, keep in St st throughout), work to last st in Row 1 of Cross St, k1 (seam st, keep in St st throughout).
Cont as est working Rows 2–8 of Cross St and seam sts in St st.
Next row: (WS) Loosely BO all sts knitwise.
Sew back neck.

Begin band for cuff
With dpns, at lower edge of sleeve with RS facing, pick up and knit 30 (32, 33, 33, 34, 35, 37, 38, 42) sts along one side of sleeve, then 30 (32, 33, 33, 34, 35, 37, 38, 42) sts along the other side—60 (64, 66, 66, 68, 70, 74, 76, 84) sts. Join to work in the rnd, pm for BOR.

Begin garter stitch
First rnd: Purl.
Next rnd: Knit.
Next rnd: Purl.
Next rnd: Loosely BO all sts knitwise.

Repeat on second sleeve.

ABBREVIATIONS & TECHNIQUES

approx: approximately

beg: begin(ning)

BO: bind off

BOR: beginning of round

circ: circular

CO: cast on

cont: continue

dec('d): decrease(d)

dpns: double-pointed needles

est: establish(ed)

inc('d): increase(d)

k: knit

k1-f/b: knit into front and back of next st (1 st increased)

k2tog: knit 2 sts together (1 st decreased)

LH: left hand

m: marker

m1-L (make 1 left slanting): Insert left needle from front to back under horizontal strand between st just worked and next st, knit lifted strand through the back loop (1 st increased)

m1-R (make 1 right slanting): Insert left needle from back to front under horizontal strand between st just worked and next st, knit lifted strand through the front loop (1 st increased)

meas: measure(s)

p: purl

p2tog: Purl 2 sts together (1 st decreased).

p2tog-tbl: Purl 2 sts together through the back loops (1 st decreased)

pc: piece(s)

pm: place marker

rem: remain

rep: repeat

rnd: round

RH: right hand

RS: right side

sl: slip

sl—k2tog—psso: Slip 1 st knitwise, k2tog, pass slipped st over st created by k2tog (2 sts decreased).

ssk (slip, slip, knit): Slip 2 sts one at a time knitwise to the right needle; return sts to left needle in turned position and knit them together through the back loops (1 st decreased)

ssp (slip, slip, purl): Slip 2 sts one at a time knitwise to the right needle; return sts to left needle in turned position and purl them together through the back loops (1 st decreased)

st(s): stitch(es)

St st: stockinette stitch

WS: wrong side

wyib: with yarn in back

yo: yarn over

Backward loop cast on
*Wrap yarn around left thumb from front to back and secure in palm with other fingers. Insert needle upwards through strand on thumb. Slip loop from thumb onto right needle, pulling yarn to tighten; rep from * for indicated number of sts.

Sunday Short Rows
http://www.sundayknits.com/techniques/shortrows.html

Long-tail cast on
http://www.knitty.com/ISSUEsummer05/FEAT-sum05TT.html

Provisional cast on
http://www.knitty.com/ISSUEfall05/FEATfall05TT.html

Stockinette stitch flat
Knit on RS, purl on WS.

Stockinette stitch in the rnd
Knit every rnd.

Garter stitch flat
Knit every row.

Garter stitch in the rnd
Rnd 1: Purl.
Rnd 2: Knit.
Rep Rnds 1 and 2 for garter st in the rnd.

About...

Carrie Bostick Hoge is a photographer and designer who lives on a lush-green acre in Maine with her family, cats, and chickens. She helped get the yarn company Quince & Co. off the ground and worked there as Art Director, Photographer, and Knitwear Designer from 2010 to 2013. She now has fun working on Madder patterns in her backyard barn-studio. Carrie's designs have been published in *Interweave Knits, Knitscene,* Brooklyn Tweed's *Wool People, New England Knits, Fair Isle Style,* and *Taproot Magazine.*

www.maddermade.com

For...

My mom, who continually supports me in all that I do.
I love you.

And, Pam Allen. Thank you for being an amazing mentor,
a great friend, and forever my two-mama (as Imogen once
called you).

Thanks...

A special thank you to: Cecily Glowik MacDonald for always helping
me when I ask for favors. Hannah Fettig, for her valued advice. Jen-
nifer Muller for her guidance on graphics. And, Bristol Ivy for her
keen proofing eyes.

The talented knitters: Sue Macurdy, Nicole Dupuis, Lori Ann Gra-
ham, Peter Kennedy, Cecily Glowik MacDonald, Allie Matthews, and
Larisa Norman.

The trusty tech editors: Kristen TenDyke & Dawn Catanzaro.

The beautiful models: Chloe Cekada, Ashley Letizia, and my darling
goose, Imogen Amelia.

And thank you to all the lovely readers of my blog who leave positive
and encouraging comments... I'm lucky to have you.

xo
carrie